Bible Truth
about
DELIVERANCE

Bible Truth about DELIVERANCE

PASTOR YEMI ADEDEJI, MD

ISBN: 978-1-64970-030-8   (Paperback Edition)
ISBN: 978-1-64970-033-9   (Hardcover Edition)
ISBN: 978-1-64970-029-2   (E-book Edition)

Book Ordering Information

Phone Number: 347-901-4929 or 347-901-4920
Email: info@globalsummithouse.com
Global Summit House
www.globalsummithouse.com

Printed in the United States of America

Introduction

Depending on the school of thought, there are a lot of stories and myths that revolve around the topic of deliverance or as some call it exorcism. From heathen cultures to conservative theology, deliverance is a topic that is often sought but seldom understood. Ranging from sickness to lack, misfortune and limitation in an area of life or sudden and even tragic death, there are those who believe that deliverance is the solution to every problem in life. On the other hand, the conservative Christian shuns the rituals of active deliverance sessions but believes that the word of God, precisely the teachings of the New Testament is all that's needed to solve every problem in life because Jesus has delivered those who believe from the curse of the law and has made them into new creatures. Many who adhere to this latter view usually do not accept that the Old Testament has much relevance today, except for its historical value.

As one who has been in active ministry for greater than twenty five years, I desire in a nutshell to reveal to the prudent my observation and experience on this controversial topic in light of the Word of God, both the Old and the New Testament, with the hope that the Bible truth will set the record straight and prevent many from deception or denial. Remember that "you shall know the Truth and that Truth shall make you Free." John 8:32

Prayer for Insight and Understanding

Dear God (if you're born again, you have the right to address God as Father),

There is a reason why You have allowed me to have access to this book. I ask in humility that You cause my heart to understand the message that You have for me through this book. May Your Spirit of truth enlighten and instruct me in truth and righteousness while removing any unjust indoctrination and ideology that has or will hinder me from living a life of freedom. In Jesus name I ask with thanksgiving for the answers. Amen!

Contents

Chapter One

Deliverance

Deliverance by definition is the action of setting free or to escape from peril. It implies to save (rescue) from danger and to liberate (set loose) from bondage. Salvation means to escape from danger while libration means to set free or to release from bondage. A person who is in danger needs to be rescued or saved. Just imagine a person who can't swim falling into the deep end of a pool. He will drown unless someone who can swim jumps in to the pool and rescues him. Or imagine someone trapped in a burning house. Death is eminent unless a fireman reaches him in time. These are illustrations of the act of salvation and salvation is only one aspect of deliverance. The other side to deliverance is the component of liberation or setting free. For example, birds are caged by owners so that they do not fly away. While in the cage, the owner feeds the bird when he wants and treats the bird in a manner dependent on why he has caged the bird. No matter how much the owner loves the bird and takes care of it, the bird is still in the bondage of the cage. The bird's life and productivity is limited due to the confinement. As will be discussed later, the purpose of bondage otherwise known as enslavement, is to cause predetermined limitation. Interestingly, the Bible reveals that as a bird can be caged, so also the soul of a man can be caged (Psalm 124:7). A man whose soul has been cage will look physically like everyone else, but unfortunately, this man will be limited in many areas of his life. The work of deliverance will open the cage and set the soul free to live a life without limitation.

Jesus Christ asked believers to pray to the Father as follow; "And do not lead us into temptation, but deliver us from evil." Matt. 6:13. The writer of Hebrews asked, "how shall we escape if we neglect so great a salvation…?" Heb.2:3. Deliverance therefore means to be saved from visible and invisible danger or evil. In Matthew 14: 28-30, Peter requested Master Jesus to command him to walk on water, which the Master did. After a few steps on the water, while observing the surrounding wind, Peter became afraid and then began to sink. He was not in any type of bondage, but he was in danger. Knowing he could not help himself, Peter cried out saying, "Lord, save me". In other words, "Lord, deliver me from this evil". The Master then reached out and saved him. You see, deliverance implies rescue or salvation from evil. Evil has different forms and comes in different shapes and sizes. Evil may be natural or supernatural. It may be spiritual, emotional or physical. Consider the words of Joseph, son of Jacob. He was sold into slavery by his brothers and after about 13 years of hardship the Lord uplifted him to second in command in Egypt. Eventually Joseph was re-united with his brothers after many years and he explained to them that what they meant for evil, God turned around for good. Listen to his words;

> *But now, do not therefore be grieved or angry with*
> *Yourselves because you sold me here; For God sent*
> *Me before you to preserve life.*
> *For these two years the famine has been in the land,*
> *And there are still five years in which there will be*
> *Neither plowing nor harvesting.*
> *And God sent me before you to preserve a posterity*
> *for you in the earth, and to <u>save your lives by a great*
> *deliverance.</u>*

> **Gen. 45:5-7**

The deliverance the Joseph was referring to was from the devastation of famine and poverty. You can be delivered from lack, and suffering not necessary caused by devils or demons, but by natural circumstances. You can be delivered from accidents and pestilence. As long as God provides a channel of escape from danger and destruction, that is deliverance.

Everyone who is not born again is in danger of God's wrath and the judgment of hell fire. If you're not born again, you need to be saved. This is the ultimate deliverance. Forget about the need of deliverance from devils, demons and bondages if you're not yet born again. The greatest deliverance is salvation from sin which will provoke the heated wrath of God on humanity and the universe as we know it. Jesus came to save mankind from their sin (Matt. 1:21). Slavery to sin permits every type of bondage and entrapment to overtake you. But once the sin issue is settled and you are at peace with God, unlimited potential for freedom from all yoke and devastation is attainable. Listen to Jesus;

> *Then Jesus said to those Jews who believed in Him,*
> *"If you abide in My word, you are My disciples indeed.*
> *And you shall know the truth and the truth shall make*
> *you free." They answered Him, "We are Abraham's*
> *descendants, and have never been in bondage to anyone.*
> *How can you say, 'you shall be made free'?" Jesus*
> *answered them, "Most assuredly, I say to you, whoever*
> *commits sin is a slave of sin. And a slave does not abide*
> *in the house forever, but a son abides forever. Therefore*
> *if the Son makes you free, you shall be free indeed."*
>
> *John 8:31-36*

From the dialogue in this text, Jesus' audience understood that a person only required freedom if he was in bondage or if he was enslaved and because they were not slaves to anyone, they resent Jesus' implication that they were in bondage. But Jesus' contention was that they all needed liberation because they were slaves to sin and the only remedy was for the Son (who was already free) to liberate them from their yokes. Freedom therefore means to be released from bondage or limitations. So while salvation is an escape from danger, liberation is a release from spiritual, emotional or physical limitation, yoke, bondage, enslavement and entrapment.

Deliverance is not passive, it is an action. It is not an abstract reaction. It is an entity of impact. Deliverance, when and if it occurs cannot go unnoticed, rather it always produces a change in the life of the person who has been delivered. Deliverance changes a person's state of wellbeing, his circumstance and situation. It produces a manifestation. When the young slave girl was delivered by Paul from the spirit of divination which possessed her, she lost her ability to foretell (Acts. 16:16-19). When Jesus delivered the epileptic boy from the deaf and dumb spirit that possessed him, the boy convulsed greatly and then fell down as if dead (Mk. 9:25-27). Anytime deliverance occurs there is an almost instantaneous sign that will confirm that a change has occurred. At times this confirmation is observed through dreams and vision depending on the channel through which deliverance occurred. More will be said later on the various channels of deliverance. When Joseph received deliverance from the yoke of hardship and slavery, his address changed from the prison to the palace. If you've been under a yoke of heavy burden as Joseph, your prison door will open and your address will change in Jesus name.

There is no need for deliverance unless one is in bondage or enslavement. But there is a need to actively and consciously maintain your freedom and liberty after you have been delivered from sin, evil or the powers of darkness. We live in a world today that has passed through eras of slavery, apartheid, segregation, discrimination and abuse of one race by another or even of one nation over the other. When the suppressed race or nation breaks free or is released from the tyrannical influence of the suppressor, deliverance has taken place. Whether it is by legislature or by raw force, the suppressed has obtained license to live outside of the influence of the suppressor. This slavery concept is also demonstrated when an individual is under mental, emotional and physical influence of suppression because of circumstances that are out of his control. Agony and torment are the results of suppression, no matter the type. Once delivered, you must keep away from the environment or individuals or the influence that suppressed your potentials and the essence of your existence or else you will return to square one. When Israel was delivered from Egypt, the house of bondage, they were commanded never to associate with the Egyptians forever. This was to guarantee that their freedom would be maintained. People who are in bondage to substances such as alcohol, drugs or sex, once delivered should not go near the enslaving influence for fear of re-entrapment.

> **Stand fast therefore in the liberty by which Christ has made us free**
> **And do not be entangled again with a yoke of bondage.**
> **Galatians 5:1**

Knowledge & Wisdom

You do what you do because of who you are. You are who you are because of how you think. You think the way you think because of what you know or what you were taught. A doctor, engineer, lawyer, politician, sorcerer etc are who they are by virtue of acquired knowledge. Indoctrination or in simple terms, the influence of "knowledge" makes you who you are. It affects your perception, thought and consequently, what you do or cannot do. Hence the scriptures;

1. "My people are destroyed for lack knowledge…" Hosea 4:6

2. "My people have gone into captivity because they have no knowledge…" Isaiah 5:13

3. "And you shall know the truth and the truth shall make you free..." John 8:32

I define knowledge is the acquisition of relevant information. Know is revelation and is therefore potentially powerful. It is like a key that unlocks doors, chains, gates, padlocks and whatever can be locked. It has the potential to produce freedom. As there are many locks so are there many keys. Every lock has its unique key. So for knowledge to produce an effective result, it must be applied in the right context and situation. This is wisdom. Wisdom is the rightful application of knowledge. It implies using the right key for the right lock, discerning difference and understanding purpose. As much as knowledge is critical, wisdom is superior and should be engaged in the act of deliverance. "Wisdom is better than strength (knowledge or potential power)" Ecclesiastes 9:16. And of course, "Wisdom is the principal thing; therefore get wisdom…" Proverbs 4:7.

Your next question should be, "how can I obtain wisdom"? By going to Princeton, Harvard, Yale, Oxford or University of Ibadan? Unfortunately, all who go to these wonderful and historic institutions pay a lot of money to get knowledge and respect, but few come out with genuine wisdom. Wisdom is not birth from experience alone, but also from an internal fabric of man that even philosophers find difficult to explain. The purpose of wisdom is to solve problems (or produce deliverance). Everyone can cause problems. Only few can solve problems. It is therefore obvious that wisdom abides in the heart, not in the brain as does knowledge. It is spiritual. Because it is spiritual, you cannot buy it. Thankfully, it can be acquired by measures or by following divine protocol and prescription.

The Bible illustrates various individuals who exhibited wisdom. Most prominent are Joseph (Gen. 41:25-36), David (1 Sam. 18:5), Daniel and his friends (Dan. 1:19-20), Abigail (1 Sam. 25:3), Solomon (1 Kg. 3:12), Prince of Tyre (Ezek. 28: 3-4), Satan (Ezek. 28:12), Ahithophel (2 Sam. 16:23). From these references, it can be concluded that there are godly wisdom and evil wisdom. Godly wisdom brings solutions and opens doors of peace and prosperity while satanic or sensual wisdom creates problems and fosters sin. It is also certain that wisdom is given as a virtue in measures. Daniel and Solomon asked for it and God gave it to them. James encourages anyone who lacked wisdom to ask God and he shall be given (James 1:5).

Jesus

Wisdom personified is Jesus the Christ. He is the wisdom of God for man. "To those who are called, Christ is the power of God and the wisdom of God" (1 Cor. 1:24, 30). True and complete deliverance begins with Him and He alone can deliver from the cause and effect of enslavement. To establish this fact, He declares to all, "therefore, if the Son makes you free, you shall be free indeed" (John 8:36). Accepting Jesus as your Lord and Savior is the single most important thing you need to do to initiate your deliverance process. The root cause of danger and bondage is sin. In the Adamic era sin was an option, not a nature. Adam and Eve had a choice and they choose to disobey God by listening to the devil. The choice they made separated them from God's presence and fellowship, neutralized the blessing and emphasized the curse.

> *Do you not know that to whom you present yourselves slaves to obey, you are that ones slave, whom you obey, whether of sin leading to death, or of obedience leading to righteousness? Romans 6:16*

The consequence of sin is bondage, death and destruction. After the original sin, sin became a nature for everyone born through Adam and Eve, no longer an option. Sin now dominated mankind's behavior and became a way of life and part of the DNA of every human being. The dominance of sin is the nature of sin. The heart of man became deceitful and desperately wicked (Jeremiah 17:9). Then Jesus came on the scene. He was **not** born with the nature of sin but with the option to sin like Adam. Nevertheless, He chose not to sin while Adam chose to sin. He did not have the nature of sin because He was born of a virgin, not by the union of a man and a woman. The virgin birth provided Jesus with a human body but not a human nature. What the breathe of God did for Adam to make him a living soul was replicated by the Holy Spirit as it overshadowed Mary, bringing about conception of a holy child without the blemish of sin. Thus Jesus became the last Adam, the life giving Spirit (1 Corinthians 15:45). Faith in Jesus guarantees not so much a change in your physical appearance, but a spiritual transformation that converts the believer into a new creation in which the nature of sin is destroyed (2 Corinthians 5:17). To experience this unique transformation, you must confess Jesus as your Lord and Savior. Go ahead, if you've never done so before. Repeat the following boldly out loud now;

Dear God. I believe that Jesus is the second Adam, the life giving Spirit, the only worthy Son of God Who died for the sins of the world and was raised to life again. I welcome you, Jesus into my deceitful and wicked heart. Forgive me of my sins and destroy my indwelling Adamic nature of sin. Deliver me from all the consequences of sin and empower me to live the God kind of life on this earth. In Jesus name I pray. Amen!

If your prayed this simple prayer in faith (Romans 10:9-10), consider yourself saved from all the consequences sin, which includes the wrath of God the will be demonstrated on the disobedient and the potential to live a life of freedom and peace. Congratulations.

This is your master key for any lock of enslavement. Am I saying that unbelievers and pagans cannot be delivered? No. I would be naïve to say that. For example, the pagan girl with the spirit of divination in Acts 16:16-18 was delivered by Paul the Apostle. Depending on the type of bondage or enslavement, non-believers in Jesus Christ may obtain temporal liberation by using medication, counseling, prayer, ritual and even yoga. But without Jesus in their heart, the root cause of slavery can never be eliminated because the sin issue has not been dealt with. And only Jesus can adequately deal with sin. His unblemished blood was shed in death for this purpose. Since you've accept Jesus, you've become a child of God and His DNA is now grafted into yours. Sin does not have dominion over you any longer (Romans 6:12-14). You have a choice. Choose not to sin. Choose righteousness. Jesus came to save and deliver the world in general but you in particular. He came to set even the lawful captive free.

Chapter Two

Purpose Of Enslavement

Enslavement simply means to be brought into captivity. To be a victim or to be treated as a slave. You may not be a slave, but you are treated like one or you are made to believe that you are one. You are limited in your aspirations and inspirations. You do not see any good in yourself or in your life, even when it is clear that you have such great potentials and ability. Have you not heard or seen people who outwardly seem to have it together but yet are miserable and depressed to the point of suicidal tendencies. This is mental slavery, diminished self-esteem and emotional disorders. You can also be a slave emotionally. This occur when you cannot resist the taunting and persuasion of other person, when you are under the control of another person's command or addicted to certain substances and behaviors. Many times this emotional slavery is in the name of love, obsession or the desire to be accepted by others. Emotional slavery has led many people to become gang members, "worka-holics", addicts to drugs or to a perverse life style such as pornography and prostitution. Finally, there is physical enslavement. This is when you put great effort into a task only to become a failure over and over again. There is nothing to show for your wisdom, intelligence or eloquence. Absolutely nothing to show for all your hard work and labor. You're never in control, never in command and never on top. You're always begging your way through and even at that, nothing ever goes the way you plan. Even when you hope for the best and make plans to the best of your ability, failure is often the result. Your story is one of delays and denials continuously. It's always worse than you anticipated. Your expectations are constantly disappointed and you are never appreciated. This is the life cycle of a slave. Not until you have chains on your hands and legs are you a slave, but once you are unable to live in freedom to have what you want at the time you need it or to accomplish good things at the time it is of value, then you are a slave. Remember that as a bird can be caged so can the soul of a man be caged.

Nothing happens by chance or coincidence. There is a purpose behind every event of life. You may not know or understand that purpose, nevertheless a reason exist. Your life has a purpose and your existence has a meaning. Once you discover this, you are on the path to fulfillment. The sooner in life this self-discovery is made, the certain it is that you will accomplish all that the Lord has created you to do. In light of this you should understand that there are reasons why the enemy enslaves you. You are not enslaved because the enemy has nothing better to do with his time. Not so. The purpose of enslavement is to strategically keep you distracted from purpose, to keep you from becoming the person that God has predestined you to be and to delay God's purpose for your life for as long as possible, knowing that you have a limited amount of time to live here on earth. Many times you may be unaware of these strategies and tactics, even long after they have been set in operation. There are four reasons why you experience enslavement, limitation and devastation. These reasons are sometimes progressive and are listed as follow;

1. Frustration

2. Intimidation

3. Manipulation

4. Domination

Frustration: This is a feeling of dissatisfaction, often accompanied by anxiety or depression, resulting from unfulfilled need or unresolved problems. It is the emotional reaction that results when you are hindered from a potentially satisfying activity. Prolonged frustration will lead to a state of mental or physical breakdown, a state of hopelessness and helplessness where it appears that life is not worth living. Frustrated persons are the ones who commit suicide. A person who is fulfilled and satisfied does not want to die. Frustration is a devastating tool of the enemy to destroy your destiny. Don't give in to it. Remember that the enemy comes not but to steal, kill and destroy (John 10:10). It is your destiny that he is after. Don't let go without a fight. If you are willing to fight, with God on your side, you will no doubt win.

In Genesis 26, God commanded Isaac to dwell in a particular land called Gerar and there he will be blessed. Isaac obeyed and he received a hundred fold increase in just one year. I love how verse 13 described his blessing. "The man began to prosper, and continued to prosper until he became very prosperous." As you read on, may the God of the new covenant release an anointing for progressive prosperity upon your life in Jesus' name. There is nothing wrong with prosperity, as long as Jesus Christ is in the center of it. I believe God for yearly significant increment of prosperity in my own family life and ministry, so that others will become blessed through my blessing. Beloved, God is proving Himself to be faithful. The prosperity of Isaac exceeded that of his neighbors and that of the indigents of the land. Your prosperity will exceed that of the heathen in Jesus name. Isaac was requested to move to another territory not too far away, and he did. In the Valley of Gerar he dug up the wells that his father Abraham had dug in his days but which the Philistines had stopped after Abraham's death. There arose a quarrel between the herdsmen of Isaac and the herdsmen of the area over the wells and running water. They claimed that the waters were theirs and not Isaacs. They quarreled over the wells till the point that Isaac gave in, being a man of principle. In other words, they frustrated Isaac until he succumbed. He left behind what he labored and struggled to acquire and moved on to start all over again. This happened again and again for Isaac, but he never for once gave up. Does this sound like the story of your life? Persistent quarrel, struggle and wasted effort? If so, I command that cycle of frustration to come to an end in your life in Jesus name. Everything will now begin to work for your good. The Bible says, "you will reap in due season if you do not faint". Don't give up. Isaac refused to give up. He refused to let the enemy have the final say. They could frustrate him but they could not stop him. You will be unstoppable in the name of Jesus. Isaac dug another well which the enemy could not contest over. He had overcome evil with good. His persistence paid off. He called the name of that well Rehoboth and he said, "For now the Lord has made room for us and we shall be fruitful in the land." This is a powerful statement. The Lord had delivered him from enemy strife. There was now a distinction between Isaac and the enemies. The difference was clear. There was no controversy that Isaac was the better man. He was above opposition. The same will be your portion in Jesus name. A well is needed for sustenance. It is a reservoir of water needed for daily living in the desert land. It was needed for Isaac and his family to be fruitful in the land. So Isaac was just creating opportunities for survival and prosperity by digging the wells. He was not digging because he had nothing better to do. He was digging because the future of his family depended on the water supply. Are you also digging a reservoir that will sustain you and your family in the future? You will hit water soon in Jesus name. Maybe you have been failing your exams or cannot seem to get the job of your qualification? Maybe your business is crumbling and every attempt to advance yourself is useless? I declare to you that you are about to reach your Rehoboth in the name of Jesus. The tool you need to make you fruitful in the land shall be given to you in Jesus name. Go ahead and receive it right now!

Intimidation: This is the act of making timid or making afraid. It is the ability to force into an action or to prevent from acting by inducing fear. Intimidation is a means of discouragement. Anyone can be intimidated, not just the weak or the timid. Even the strongest and most powerful of men can be intimidated. Show me a person who is fearful and I will show you a person who can be intimidated, because fear is the agent of intimation. It is a well know fact that one of the greatest weapons of the enemy is fear. Fear is the opponent of faith. The heart is where either faith or fear is stored. At any given time, the heart can only store either faith or fear. Both cannot co-exist together but one can replace the other depending on other prevailing factors. Factors the increase faith will decrease fear in your life, while factors the increase fear will decrease faith. For instance, there is no fear in love, rather perfect love casts out fear (1John 4:18). On the other hand faith works by love (Gal. 5:6). Faith is increased by hearing the word of God while fear is increased when you stop believing the word of God and begin to accept human policies or focus on worldly circumstance.

Elijah was a man of God anointed to do great works in his days. God used him to seal up the heavens for 3 ½ years so that there will be no rain, resulting in a famine across the land. He was used to sustain the widow of Zarephath and her son by a word of command. When the son died, Elijah raised him back to life. At his beckoning the heavens were again opened and the land had rain. He challenged and defeated the 450 prophets of Baal on mount Carmel. Elijah appeared to be unstoppable until he was unexpectedly confronted by Jezebel, who sent a messenger to him threatening his life. At this critical moment, the man of faith became a man of fear. He forgot all that the Lord had accomplish through him and instead of standing up to the challenge he fled for his life because he was afraid. Jezebel succeeded in intimidating Elijah. He became discouraged. Elijah allowed intimidation to cut short his success and nearly destroyed his ministry. Do you want to leave your job because of a boss who is intimidating you? Don't. Just stay your ground prayerfully. The Lord will turn your situation around. Don't allow the enemy to intimidate you or ensnare you with fear. Stand on the word of God that is relevant to your situation. If you had a dream that scared or that intimidated you. Just stand in faith, even if you were defeated in the dream or something terrible happened such as a demonic physical and sexual assault. Remember that no one can speak a word and it comes to pass except the Lord has spoken it. Only the living God can say a word and bring it to manifestation without man's ability to override it. Only God can do a thing and no one can reverse it. Even satan and his cohorts cannot override it. But whatever the enemies speak or perform against you will not come to pass unless you agree to it. If you refuse and reject it immediately, heaven will support you. The longer you wait before taking spiritual action the less likely you will be able to reverse the forces that have been set in motion.

David stood up to the taunting of Goliath when no one else would. Everyone was afraid and intimidated by the presence of this giant, but not David (1 Sam. 17:10-11). David kept his focus on God not on the giant. His faith in Jehovah was firm. He refused to be intimidated. He knew that his God was bigger than Goliath. Even when Goliath cursed him, David retaliated with words that were more demeaning to Goliath. David had the last word, not Goliath. You should have the last word in the challenges that you face. Never let the opponent have the last word. When you speak, make sure you speak in the name of the Lord your God and let it be known that you represent Him and it is He Who will fight the battle for you. David said, "You come to me with a sword, with a spear and with a javelin. But I come to you in the name of the Lord of Hosts, the God of the armies of Israel, whom you have defiled. "This day the Lord will deliver you into my hand and I will strike you and take your head from you" (1Sam. 17:45-46). When you believe that it is God who will fight for you, no one can intimidate you. No one can stop you. I pray for you right now that every power that has been intimidating you up till now will fail in the name of Jesus. Every situation that has made you to be a grasshopper in the land of abundance instead of the giant that God wants you to be, will change right from this moment in the name of Jesus. You will not be lesser than who God has made you.

Manipulation: To negotiate, to control or influence someone cleverly, skillfully or deviously. In the context of the enemy's objective to manipulate you, it is usually by deception. The end result of manipulation is to take something very precious away from you or to disqualify you from your rightful entitlement. Instead of forceful and open confrontation, the enemy is subtle and pretentious in his approach. In many instances manipulation is a process that occurs gradually over a period of time. That is the enemy first develops a relationship of trust with the victim, before executing his plan. By the act of seduction Delilah persistently enticed Samson until he was persuaded to reveal the secret of his strength to her, thereby bringing the mighty man into captivity and shame. Delilah agreed to bring down Samson for her own financial gain. She did not care what happened to him, but was only concerned about herself (Judges 16). By her persistence she was able to enslave and destroy the life and ministry of a great man of God. Samson's weakness and lustful desires were used to manipulate him.

He loved Delilah and consequently developed a relationship of trust with her. He would never have guessed that she would stab him in the back. This is true up until today. The enemy will befriend you in order to harm you. Therefore, choose your friends carefully and prayerfully. There are not many people that you can trust with your secrets. Be very careful of those you choose to reveal your secrets to.

The man of God in 1st Kings Chapter 13 made this mistake as well. After a great victory over king Jeroboam in front of the Temple altar, the king invited him to his house perhaps to show gratitude for restore his withered hand. The man of God replied as follow;

> *"If you were to give me half your house, I would not go in with you; nor would I eat bread, nor drink water in this place.*
> *For so it was commanded me by the word of the LORD, Saying, You shall not eat bread nor drink water, nor Return by the same way you came."*
> *So he went another way and did not return by the way He came to Bethel. 1 Kings 13:8-9*

You would think that this was the end of the story, a happy victorious ending. But not so, the enemy constantly pursues seeking for opportunities to carry out his plans. And many times his plans are initiated through the least suspected channels. Unfortunately for this man of God, an old prophet lived in that city who heard of the exploits God did through this nameless man of God. You would expect the influence of the older more experienced prophet to be edifying for this man of God. On the contrary, their connection brought about doom for the man of God who revealed his secret to someone he though could be trusted. The old prophet being more experienced persuaded the man of God to unknowingly rebel against the instructions that the LORD had given him for the assignment. This old prophet spoke in the name of the LORD. Consider their conversation;

Then he said to him, come home with me and eat bread.

And he replied, I may not return with you nor go home with you: neither will I eat bread nor drink water with you in this place:

For it was said to me by the word of the Lord, you shall not eat bread nor drink water there, nor turn again to go by the way you came.

He said to him, I am a prophet also as you are; and an angel spoke to me by the word of the LORD, saying, bring him back with you to your house that he may eat bread and drink water. But he lied to him.

So he went back with him, and did eat bread in his house, and drank water.

And it came to pass, as they sat at the table, that the word of the LORD came unto the prophet that brought him back.

And he cried to the man of God that came from Judah, saying, This is what the LORD says, forasmuch as you have disobeyed the mouth of the Lord, and have not kept the commandment that the LORD gave you,

But came back and have eaten bread and drunk water in the place of which the LORD said to you not to eat no bread or drink no water, your carcass shall not come into the sepulcher of your fathers.

1 Kings 13:15-22

The man of God from Judah was manipulated through deception and was ultimately destroyed. He was made to do something he would not ordinarily do based on his conviction. The enemy continues to devise strategies of manipulation to destroy the unsuspecting. Nowadays, social addictions to sex and drugs are prevailing all over the world. The attraction for many is fame and fortune. Your prospective boss or producer or manager would encourage you to engage in certain activities, join certain clubs or keep silent about your faith in order to move up in the world. While you think you are doing the right thing, you are unknowingly being manipulated and consequently entangled in yokes that will inevitably lead to destruction.

The serpent deceived Eve in the Garden of Eden and manipulated her loyalty to God. Manipulation is the forerunner of domination. It serves to bring you under the control of another. It is a subtle chain place around your neck so that you can be limited. Once you're successfully manipulated, you will then be dominated. Sorcery and witchcraft are tested tools of manipulation. Jezebel by manipulation took the vineyard of Naboth for Ahab her husband and had Naboth wrongfully killed (1 King 21: 1-15). Simon the sorcerer manipulated the entire city of Samaria with his sorcery for a long time until the Gospel of Jesus was introduced to the people (Acts 8: 9-11). As light shines in darkness and overcomes it, the power of the Gospel of Jesus will destroy every work of manipulation in your like in Jesus name. The grip of witchcraft and socery around your life is weaken and loosen henceforth in Jesus name. Shout Halleluyah!

Domination: Means to rule, exercise control, predominate, or to occupy a commanding or elevated position. Domination also means to have power, authority or rights over another. Psalm 18:44 states "as soon as they hear of me, they shall obey me. The strangers shall submit themselves to me". The one who is being dominated submits either willing or forcefully to the one who is dominating. The ultimate purpose of enslavement is to bring you into submission again. The enemy desire to control certain areas of your life. He wants to rule over you and have you serve him. Remember the final temptations satan presented to Jesus. He showed Jesus the kingdoms of the world and their glory and then told Jesus, "all these things I will give You if You will fall down and worship me". But Jesus replied by saying, " get away from me, satan; for it is written, you shall worship the Lord your God and Him alone shall you serve". Matt. 4:8-10. Satan would have given what was in his possession to Jesus if Jesus would worship him. Remember that worship is the reverent love and devotion accorded to a deity or someone greater than yourself. The proof of worship is service. Therefore, the deity you worship is the deity you will serve. Service is then rewarded by the deity. When you worship and serve God, you are acknowledging that you love God and that he is greater than you. He will in turn bless and reward you. If you worship and serve satan, he will also reward you, or rather destroy you. Romans 6:16 states that you are the servant of whosoever you yield yourself to obey. Satan knows this all too well. He promised Jesus the reward of the glories of the world if He would worship him. If Jesus had obeyed and worshiped satan, Jesus would be declaring that He loved satan and that satan was greater than God, because you can only serve one master at a time. He would therefore become a servant of satan, if He had yielded Himself to obey him. Thank God, instead of worship, Jesus rebuked satan and he fled.

Satan continues to seek those who would yield themselves to him in worship and in service. Once you obey, no matter the reward he gives you, you are under his dominion. You're then his slave. Getting in is easy but coming out is far more difficult. It takes the intervention of He that is greater than satan to free you from his dominion. The story of Samson and Delilah in Judges Chapter 16, illustrates the process of enslavement well. The lords of the Philistines sought a way to destroy Samson because of the devastation he had caused in the cities. If you, like me, are a threat to satan's kingdom, please be on guard. There is an organized conspiracy against the lives of God's generals worldwide. My confidence is in this word, "faithful is He that called me". He has spoken concerning me, "touch not My anointed and do My prophet no harm". As I stand firm in Him, He will keep me secured until my duty is accomplished. I will fight a good fight and I will finish my course. The struggles of the righteous may be many, but God will deliver him out of them all.

Delilah agreed to seduce and betray Samson into the hand of the lords of the Philistines, who would lavishly reward her. The Philistines had observed that Samson had a weakness for women, especially foreign women. It became obvious that it would be through this weakness that they would destroy him. Beware, child of God. Everyone has a weakness or weaknesses. It may be sin or just an area of compromise. You should identify your weakness and make every effort to overcome it. If not, this will be the primary area of attack from the enemy. Weaknesses create doorways for enslavement. Samson eventually gave in to the pressure of Delilah. Once his Nazarene vow was broken, Samson was at the mercy of the enemy. They took him, put out his eyes, bound him imprisoned him and made him to serve hard labor in the enemy's prison. Samson was no longer free but under the dominion of his enemies. Beloved, I pray that your glorious life will not end up like that of Samson. You will not fall into deception nor will you be dominated by the enemy in Jesus name.

Chapter Three

Doorways To Enslavement

A doorway allows for entrance or exit. In the case of enslavement, doorways represent factors that make you susceptible to the domination of the enemy or that gives the enemy access to intimidate, frustrate, manipulate and dominate you. These doorways are mainly your attitudes and actions that attract or enhance the operation of the enemy in your life. There are many doorways exhibited by which the enemy may reach in and operate on you or through you. Hebrews 12:1 puts it this way; "let's lay aside every weight and the sin that easily besets us". Sin of all types are doorways that grant the enemy permission to attack and carry out their enterprises. Sins are obvious behaviors while weights are not so obvious. Weights are not necessarily evil but represents appearances of evil. Besetting weights include but are not limited to being unequally yoked with unbelievers, lack of moderation in dressing and outward appearance, use of alcohol and tobacco, listening to worldly music and going to places that may compromise your faith. Doorways may therefore be created by excess weight that in comparison, slows down a runner or a habitual sin that leads to destruction. Sin is a reflection of disobedience and all forms of disobedience to the will of God have spiritual and physical consequences. If you're willing and obedient you will eat the good of the land, but if you refuse and rebel, you shall be devoured by the sword (Isa. 1:19-20). So beloved, understand that not all doorways are sin. Some are weights designed to slow you down, distract or confuse you. Some of these weights are unchecked negative human nature which do not align with the nature of God. A child of God ought to have the genes of God. First John 3:9, confirms that whoever is born of God cannot continue to sin because God's seed (genes) dwells in him. God's seed is God's word. As you feed on the truth of God's word, your mind becomes renewed and you become transformed. Let's now consider a few selected weights and sin in light of the doorway they create in a person's life.

Rebellion and Stubbornness: First Samuel 15:23 states that rebellion is as the sin of witchcraft and stubbornness is as idolatry. If you have a stubborn or rebellious attitude, you are susceptible to the practice of witchcraft and idolatry. Saul the king possessed these traits and he eventually sought after assistance from the witch of Endor (1 Sam. 28:7). Rebellion paves the way for destruction and tragic death (Isaiah 1:20). Stubbornness is hardness of heart. It leads to lack of discernment and unforgiveness. When you fail to release others who have offended you by not forgiving them, you also hold yourself bound and hinder your own prayers as well. The scriptures therefore admonishes us to forgive so that our prayers may be answered (Mark 11:24-26).

Envy and Hatred: Because Saul was envious of David, hatred developed in his heart towards David. The Spirit of God left him and an evil spirit possessed him (1 Sam. 18:9-10). If unchecked, hatred will develop in the heart of the envious. Hatred will then lead to other forms of sin such as lies, anger, robbery and murder. Josephs' brothers hated him and therefore conspired to kill him.

Greed and Selfishness: When you are too pre-occupied with self, you will do anything to get what you want at any given time, you are treading on dangerous lines. You have opened the door for satan to enter and use you as an instrument. Gehazi was greedy for the spoils of Namaan (2 Kings 5:20-21). Ahab was greedy for Naboth vineyard (1

Kings 21), David had an uncontrollable desire for Bathsheba, Uriah's wife (2 Samuel 11). Judas was a thief. He did not hesitate to betray his Master for money (Luke 22:3-6).

Fear and Unbelief: The fearful and unbelieving are unstable. You run when no one is chasing you and you are easily intimidated, indoctrinated and manipulated. I John 4:18 declares that "fear has torment". The more fearful you are the more vulnerable you are. The more you doubt, the more you drown (Matthew 14:30) and the less you will receive from God (James 1:6-7).

Negative Confessions: Words are creative on the one hand and destructive on the other hand. When you speak positively, you create a positive atmosphere but when you speak negatively, you create a negative atmosphere (Prov. 18:21, 2 Samuel 1:15-16). Words can heal and words can kill. Every idle or unnecessary spoken word shall be judged. Satan can use you confessions to destroy you or your loved ones. The words you speak portray your level of understanding as well as the thoughts of your heart. Out of the abundance of the heart, the mouth speaks. A man of faith will speak words of faith. A perverse man will speak perversion. God assesses you by your words and so does satan.

Pride: This is the opposite of a humble spirit. Pride was first described in lucifer, who desired to be above every other angel and be like the Most High (Isaiah 14: 12-14). He subsequently fall. Pride always precedes a fall while humility precedes promotion (Prov. 16:18, James 4:10). Herod's pride hastened his destruction (Acts 12: 20-23). Pride is not submissive at all. It is rebellious and constantly pursuing that which belongs to another. Absalom could not submit to his father David. Instead he want to be king in his place and have people serve him (2 Samuel 15). He end was tragic and sudden destruction. Pride occurs when you see yourself as being better than others or more privileged than others, when you attribute your abilities, achievements and possessions to your works rather than God's grace. Just keep in mind that God resists the proud but gives grace to the humble (1 Peter 5:5).

Association: This is an organization of individuals with a common purpose or agreement. Friendships, cults and soul ties proceed from associations. When you unite yourself with someone else in a physical, business, sexual or spiritual agreement, you are bound to share in the properties that make up the life of that person. "Evil communications spoil good manners" and "be not unequally yoked together with unbelievers", are scriptures that warn us of the devastating power that is in associating with the wrong person. Among other things, your dreams will reveal to you clearly if you are in a wrong association. The enemy may use the one you associate with to enslave you if you are not discerning (Psalm 106:35-36). King Asa began to backslide after his association with Benhadad (2 Chronicles 16:2-4), King Jehoshaphat nearly lost his life because of his commitment to King Ahab to unite in battle in order to regain Ramoth-Gilead for Ahab (2 Chronicles 18:31-32). Therefore, beware. As you will later see, associating with the right person may bring you deliverance.

Righteous Living: Obviously, this is not a weight nor a sin, but righteous living can also open the door for the attack of the enemy. This form of attack may not necessarily lead to enslavement. Psalm 34:17-19 says that the righteous cry out to God because of their many troubles and afflictions. The Lord's promise is to deliver him out of them all. Being righteous and God fearing attracts problems. It attracts attacks from satanic agents assigned to destroy or limit your influence and achievement. Everyone who will live godly will suffer persecution. The attacks may come from sources far away and unknown, or may come from those closest to you like in the case of Abel the son of Adam and Joseph the son of Jacob. Paul and Silas were busy doing the Lord's assignment for their lives when they were wrongfully punished and imprisoned. When you find yourself in such situations, James and Peter admonish you to rejoice (James 1:2, 1 Peter 4:12-13). Once you are identified as a potential threat to the kingdom of darkness, you are placed on satan's hit list in order to neutralize or nullify your effectiveness against his works in your life and that of others. Another trick of the devil is to get the righteous distracted and confused. He achieves this mainly by deception. He may cause a righteous lady to get involved with a terrible man who she will spend half her life praying for his change of heart and behavior. The devil has you preoccupied with issues of little essence instead of you touching lives around you for better. How many righteous have fallen into satan's net of distraction and preoccupation. David was caught off guard when he fell for Bathsheba (2 Samuel 11:2-4).

Chapter Four

Mechanisms Of Enslavement

One of the philosophical definitions of the word "mechanism" is, a structure having an influence over the behavior of a person and in Engineering language it is defined as something resembling a machine in the arrangement and working of its parts. For lack of a better explanation, I use the word mechanism to illustrate the working parts of enslavement and its influence over a person's behavior. As with the purpose for enslavement, there are also four mechanisms by which enslavement occur. The causes of each form are also explained but always remember that even the righteous are often afflict by the enemy. Job was an upright and God fearing man when satan was permitted to attack his life and that of his loved ones. Therefore do not be presumptuous or judgmental about a person under satanic attack. Seek to answer as many questions as possible without assuming error on the victim's part unless revealed by the Holy Spirit.

Obsession: This is the constant preoccupation with a fixed idea or an unwanted feeling or emotion, often accompanied by symptoms of anxiety. King Saul was jealous of David and became obsessed with the idea of killing him (1 Samuel 18: 9-11, 28). His motivation was demonic but he ultimately was responsible for his actions. Similarly, King Ahab was greedy and consequently became obsessed with owning

Naboth vineyard. The emotion was so intense that he became sick when Naboth rejected his offer of exchange of another vineyard for his. Ahab's obsession led to a conspiracy to kill Naboth in order to take possession of his vineyard (1 Kings 21). Amnon the son of David was so obsessed with his half sister Tamar, that he became sick. Obsession led him to conspire to rape her, damning the consequences (2 Samuel 13). Obsession is a strong emotional hunger that may lead to sickness if it is not gratified. It can lead you to steal, kill and indulge in improper sexual acts. On a lighter note, some people are obsessed with eating food or with shopping unnecessarily. No one is born to be obsessive. Obsession may be as a result of a curse or as a result of willful disobedience to refrain from what you know is wrong. When your desires become uncontrolled, it becomes obsessive and you become conditioned to the feeling. Obsession often times lead to addictions. In the language of Romans 1:21-28, we may summarize as thus;

> *And even as they did not like to retain God in their knowledge, God*
> *Gave them over to a debased mind, to do those things which are not fitting.*

> *Rom. 1:28*

Causes: Lack of self control, lack of contentment and greed (covetousness), selfishness, lack of reverence for God, idolatry. People with such character are prone to be influence by demons of obsession.

Those who are obsessed should pray against the spirit of Ahab and Jezebel, as well as the spirit of Amnon and Judas. Say with boldness and authority; Every obsessive and compulsive spirit operating in my life, listen to the word of God, "all things are lawful unto me but not all things are helpful, I will not be brought under the power of any (Romans 6:12)" controlling spirit in the name of Jesus! Pray consistently until your attitude and emotions change.

Suppression: To put a forceful end to a thing; to subdue. Suppression means to curtail or prohibit certain activities, to arrest or repress. Suppression is a form of limitation. When you are oppressed, you are forcefully used but when you are suppressed, you are forcefully subdued. You are held back and you are held down when suppressed. It's like being in a cage or a prison with limited access to most of the good things in life. You are under the program and agenda of the enemy. Your finances may be suppressed by activities of the devourer. Opportunities for advancement and fulfillment may elude you when you're under suppression. Deliverance is the only remedy for those under the suppressive power of the enemy.

> *Then the children of Israel did evil in the sight of the LORD, so the LORD delivered them into the hand of Midian for seven years, and the hand of Midian prevailed against Israel. Because of the Midianites, the children of Israel made for themselves dens, the caves and the strongholds which are in the mountains.*
> *So it was, whenever Israel had sown, Midianites would come up; also Amalekites and the people of the East would come up against them.*
> *Then they would encamp against them and destroy the produce of the Earth as far as Gaza, and leave no sustenance for Israel, neither sheep nor ox, nor donkey. For they would come up with their livestock and their tents, coming in*
> *As numerous as locusts; both they and the camels were without number;*
> *And they would enter the land to destroy it.*
> *So Israel was greatly impoverished because of the Midianites, and the*
> *Children of Israel cried out to the LORD.*
>
> *Judges 6:1-6*

As you see here suppressive powers allow you to plant but then they come and destroy your harvest. They allow you to get education but will prevent you from being gainfully employed. On the other hand, you may be allowed to make a lot of money, but no matter how much you make, your expensive will always supersede your income. In 2004 I was given a job opportunity that changed my status for the better. The distance to the job was over an hour drive each way, but that didn't bother me because the money was good. I was to start on a Monday. Two days to the time, while driving to go on a weekend errand just a few blocks from where I live, my car was struck by another car that ran the stop sign and "totaled" my car. The car I depended on to get me to and from this new career opportunity. I resolved to rent a car till I was able to save enough money to buy another car. This obviously took longer than planned. The intension is to illustrate to you how these terrible powers operate to delay or prevent your harvest.

Some people have been marked by the enemy with the spirit of hatred. No matter where they go or what they do, they are not appreciated and therefore not rewarded adequately for their deeds. They are outwardly repulsive for no major reason and those who ought to assist them turn their backs at them. The enemy has sprayed their lives with a foul smelling scent such as what a skunk would do.

Causes: Lack of spiritual knowledge (Isa. 5:13), lack of prayer and discernment, lying, perversion (adultery and fornication), backsliding, failure to admit fault or to apologize, idolatry (including using charms, talisman, voodoo and juju).

Those who are being suppressed should pray against the spirit of Amalek and Midian. Say with boldness and authority: Every power of suppression that is operating in my life, listen to the word of God, "I shall be delivered from the snare of the fowler, and the lawful captive shall be delivered". Therefore, because it is written that I shall be above only, I come out from under your influence in the name of Jesus!

Oppression: To keep down by severe and unjust use of force or authority. The Egyptians oppressed the Israelites by making them serve in rigor (Exodus 1:11-14). Oppression causes unjust hardship and suffering of an individual, a family or a group of people united by culture or nationality. It results in sorrow, poverty and sickness. Oppression may be programmed for a precise time. In this case, adversity occurs to the victim at significant periods. For example, the victim may regularly fall sick on their birthday, day of an exam, interview or graduation. Others may have accidents on a specific day or month of each year. Any recurrent adversity associated with a specific period is a programmed oppression. Deliverance is the only remedy. Some individual or families are under severe oppression. They have never tasted of success, but have been moving from one level of suffering to the next. Such persons are under a yoke and burden of the enemy. A yoke is a chain or wooden bar joining the necks of two or more animals together for manual labor. A burden is a heavy load that is carried usually on the back or shoulders. People are yoked against their will. No one desires to struggle much without significant achievement to show for it. Anyone living a life of persistence struggles, constant failure or is an under achiever should be delivered from oppressive powers. Acts 10:38 confirms that God anointed Jesus with the Holy Ghost and power to do good and heal all who are oppressed by the devil. Yes the devil is the chief taskmaster of oppression and deliverance from his grips requires the intervention of the anointing of the Holy Spirit.

Causes: Stealing and corruption, lack of prayer and faith in the word of God, partiality, cheating, wickedness, shedding of innocent blood, idolatry (including using charms, talisman, voodoo and juju).

Those under oppression should pray against the spirit of the pharaoh and evil task masters. Say with boldness and authority; every power that is oppressing my life, listen to the word of God, "let My people go so they can serve me". Therefore, let me go in the name of Jesus! Let every chain and fetter used to enslave me break in the name of Jesus! Pray until your situation begins to change.

Possession: The state of being owned, controlled or dominated. As bad as it sounds to be obsessed, suppressed and oppressed, you are worst off if you are possessed. Possession involves the operation of demons from within you or the manifestation of demonic influence in your life through a covenant bond. The mind and the body now become the habitation of demons. If allowed, the ultimate objective of demons is to express their character and activities through humans. They can only achieve this by living within you. Demons desire to take over your mind and your body for the purpose of expression or affliction. A very common Biblical example is the Gadarene demoniac.

> *Then they sailed to the country of the Gadarenes, which is opposite Galilee.*
> *And when He stepped out on the land, there met Him a certain man*
> *From the city who had demons for a long time. And he wore no clothes,*
> *Nor did he live in a house but in the tombs.*
> *When he saw Jesus, he cried out, fell down before Him, and with a loud*
> *Voice said, "What have I to do with You, Jesus, Son of the Most High*
> *God? I beg You, do not torment me!"*
> *For He had commanded the unclean spirit to come out of the man. For it*
> *Had often seized him, and he was kept under guard, bound with chains*
> *And shackles; and he broke the bonds and was driven by the demon into*
> *The wilderness.*
> *Jesus asked him saying, "What is your name?" And he said, "Legion,"*
> *Because many demons had entered him.*
>
> *Luke 8:26-30*

As graphic and unbelievable as this sounds, demons can possess people in numbers, for a long period of time and alter their minds, perception of reality, and their physical strength. You may feel something moving around in your body or making sound from within you. The one who is possessed may also be a medium through which the demon spirit will operate. As the ability of becoming a medium is at times desired by some people who want to have super human abilities. They therefore mingle with the occults or idol worship, including Satanism (Acts 16:16, Leviticus 20:6, 27). Examples of mediums include soothsayers, psychics, herbalists, juju and voodoo priests, witches and sorcerers as well as those with familiar spirits. Some are mediums by desire while others are elected by the members of the society they belong and worse yet, some are assigned by relatives through covenants that they have no control over. To cease from operating as a medium, deliverance is required.

Houses and cars can also be possessed. As I will explain later, I was called upon a few years ago to expel a demon from a house in Dublin, Ireland. The demon terrorized the occupant of the family for two years and followed them from an old house to a brand new construction they purchase. I prayed in the house and anointed every door and window with oil and water. The same night the demon left the house never to return. I have also prayed over a car and even a refrigerator that were giving specific problems which defied being repaired. Prayer expelled whatever demons were in operation and the car and refrigerator worked well for some time.

Causes: Ingesting demon infested food or drink in the natural or in dreams, wet dreams, idolatry (especially family idols), involvement with the occults and false religions, prostitution, rape, blood covenants, demonic child dedications. Gang initiations lead to possession by violent evil spirit.

Those who are possessed need to be delivered. Either you seek for anointed men of God to pray for you or you should confess relevant scriptures with prayer and fasting regularly. "He sent His word and delivered them". The word of God is living and powerful (Hebrews 4:12). Proper consistent use of it will result in the cleansing of the mind and the body.

Bewitchment:

O foolish Galatians! Who has bewitched you that you should not obey the truth?

Galatians 3:1

Similar to enslavement, the purpose of bewitchment is to influence, modify or alter a person's behavior or lifestyle. The mode of operation is usually through witchcraft, sorcery or the use of occultic paraphernalia. Bewitchment is usually a calculated attempt to achieve a specific end point in the life of someone who is steadfast in the Lord. The purpose of bewitchment is to lower the divine protection around an individual through behavior modification. The outcome would be to make the righteous become unrighteous, the steadfast to become unstable and the godly to become a sinner. Bewitchment is often used when enslavement is not possible. In such cases the victim(s) is (are) first bewitched to weaken their defense and then enslavement occurs. Bewitchment usually involves close contact between the agent of bewitchment and the person or people being bewitched.

Balaam, a sorcerer, was hired by Balak the king of Moab to curse (enslave by limitation) the congregation of Israel because he was afraid that Israel would defeat him in battle and take possession of his land. Balaam was therefore given a diviner's fee to curse Israel with weakness, failure and defeat. They soon found out that Israel could not be cursed because of the overshadowing covering of God's blessing (Numbers 22 thru 24). So in order to remove the overshadowing blessing of divine protection, Balaam devise a strategy to bewitch Israel before they could be enslaved (Numbers 25:1-4, 31:16).

Solomon the son of David was a man of God, a preacher and the king of Israel. He was loyal to Jehovah for many years and thus was blessed with peace and prosperity like no other king before his time. For many years the enemy could not enslave him but as he got older he was bewitched to follow after other gods. This change of heart brought calamity to his kingdom during his lifetime and afterwards (1 Kings 11:9).

> *For it was so, when Solomon was old, that his wives*
> *turned his heart*
> *After other god; and his heart was not loyal to the*
> *LORD his God,*
> *As was the heart of his father David.*
>
> *1 Kings 11:4*

In Galatians 3:1, it is obvious that the Holy Spirit wrote through Paul the Apostle to Christians, not pagans. Something had happened to members of the Galatian Church. Some who previous obeyed the truth were now doubting and disobeying. This is behavior modification resulting from a change in attitude. The question then was posed. "Who has bewitched you"? There is a personality behind the change in attitude and behavior of these well-meaning saints. When good people change and become weary in well doing, or become complacent and luke-warm, there is usually a personality bewitching them to cause an adverse behavioral transformation. If you fall into this category, go into the presence of God seeking for fresh fire. Ask God to set ablaze the fire upon the altar of your heart. Rededicate yourself to God as soon as possible. Delay is dangerous. Make this confession:

"I bring myself under the mighty hand of God. I submit my heart to You, Lord and commit my ways to Your guidance. I refuse henceforth, to lean on my own understanding or walk according to ungodly counsel. Lord, purge my mind with Your precious blood and my affections with Your holy word. I REDEDICATE MY ENTIRE SELF TO YOU, MY GOD, IN JESUS HOLY NAME. Amen! Halleluyah!"

Consider Judas, one of the twelve chosen disciples of the Lord Jesus.

Then satan entered Judas, surnamed Iscariot, who was numbered among the twelve.

Luke 22:3.

Satan entered Judas to possess him and use him for an evil deed as explained in the Bible reference. Judas became possessed and was temporarily indwelt by satan because he walked in the way of greed. Thus greed was the doorway that lead to him being possessed by the enemy. Please note the following;

Bewitchment can change a person's behavior.
Bewitchment can destroy relationships.
Bewitchment can limit success.
Bewitchment can devour finances.
Bewitchment often precedes enslavement.

There shall not be found among you anyone who makes his son or his daughter pass through the fire, or one who practices witchcraft, or a soothsayer, or one who interprets omens, or a sorcerer, or one who conjures spells, or a medium, or a spiritist, or one who calls up the dead.

Deuteronomy 18:10-11

For rebellion is as the sin of witchcraft, And stubbornness is as iniquity and idolatry. Because you have rejected the word of the LORD, He also has rejected you from being king."

1 Samuel 15:23

> **Now it happened, when Joram saw Jehu, that he said,
> "Is it peace, Jehu?" So he answered, "What peace, as
> long as the harlotries of your mother Jezebel and her
> witchcraft are so many?"**

> **2 Kings 9:22**

> **And they caused their sons and daughters to pass
> through the fire, practiced witchcraft and soothsaying,
> and sold themselves to do evil in the sight of the LORD,
> to provoke Him to anger.**

> **2 Kings 17:17**

As mentioned earlier, witchcraft and sorcery are the essence of bewitchment. The following are some of the tools used to performed the act of bewitchment.

Spells: A series or sequence of words that have magical powers. It represents a formula that is spoken to bring another person under a satan influence. Spells are used to control another person's mind and modify their behaviors without them knowing.

Enchantments: To influence by or as if by charms and incantation. To bewitch. Magicians and people in occults use enchantments to imitate the works of the Holy Ghost. Ex. 7:11, 22, 8:7, Isa. 47:7,12. Num. 23:23

Charms: The chanting or reciting of a magic spell : incantation. A practice or expression believed to have magic power. Isa. 3:20, Ezekiel 13:18-20

Divination: The art or practice that seeks to foresee or foretell future events or discover hidden knowledge usually by the interpretation of omens or by the aid of supernatural powers. Acts 16:16

Mediums & Spiritists: Means of effecting or conveying a message or the means of transmission of a force or effect. Lev.19:31, 20:6, 27, 1Sam. 28:7,9, Isa. 8:19, 19:3.

Witchcraft: The practice of magic, especially black magic; the use of spells and the invocation of spirits. 1Sam. 15:23, 2Kg. 17:17

Sorcery: The art, practices, or spells of a person who is supposed to exercise supernatural powers through the aid of evil spirits; black magic; witchery. Num. 24:1, Acts 8:9, Gal. 5:20

Chapter Five

Dreams And Visions

Dreams and visions are the phenomenon that connects the physical world to the spiritual world. They are the primary gateway into the spirit realm. A dream is a sequence of sensations, images and thoughts occurring in a person's mind during certain stages of sleep called REM (Rapid Eye Movement) sleep cycle. This stage of sleep occurs about 90 minutes after you fall asleep and last for a few minutes alternating with another type of sleep pattern called the non-REM sleep phase. Both phases continue to alternate with the REM cycle having longer durations until you finally awake. During the REM sleep phase there is intense brain wave activity, increase heartrate, increase respiration and body movement.

Although the body is in an unconscious state, the physical observations of hyperactivity experienced during REM sleep is an indication that involuntary energy is either being received or released when you are dreaming. This exchange of energy is due to the friendly communication or hostile interaction of your soul with the spirit realm.

When this occurs in the mind of a person that is awake it is called a vision or a trance. In such a case, you are not unconscious but subconscious. The physical senses are temporarily suspended (seize) while your soul connects with the spirit realm. Seizure is a medical disorder where by the person loses control of his senses and motor functions. This loss of function is dependent on the type of seizure, whether absence seizure or grand mal seizure. It has been observed that shortly before a seizure occurs, probably within a few seconds, the person feels an aura or an overwhelming sensation before they lose control of their sensory functions, motor functions or both. I believe that this aura sensation happens when the spirit realm connects with the persons soul almost like when an appliance is plugged into an electrical socket. In a trance or vision, your eyes are typically opened but they are blind to the physical and you do not see what is in front of you. But your inner eyes, that is, your spirit man, now sees into the spirit dimension.

Dreams and visions usually carry message from the spirit world, either from God of from satan. Since dreams are more common than visions, we will focus more on dreams for now. Nevertheless, the same principles govern both. Symbols are the language of dreams and visions. Sometimes there is speech, but the majority of the time it is as if you are watching the olden day black and white silent movies. All symbols have meanings in a dream. These symbols may include houses, people, clothes, water, food, animals, trees, toys, various objects and spiritual beings. Practically everything in the physical may be represented in dreams and even some things that have no physical representation may be seen in dreams. For a better understanding, let's take a look at the spirit world.

The world of spirits is a mysterious world and for many, it's unbelievable. It comprises entities and personalities we can't see, yet which influence our daily lives. Yes, spirit beings have their own identity, names, forms and activities that differentiates them from each other, just as we find in the physical universe. Because many do not see into the spirit world, they do not completely believe in its existence. Many people, especially in the Western world, go through life declaring that there is no such thing as spirits, ghosts, angels, devils, or even God, all because they cannot see into the spirit world. Again, I say to you that because you do not see it, does not mean that it does not exist. Do they lack faith? Yes, but besides faith, they are lacking of common sense. For example, about a hundred and some years ago, if you said that there were what we call microscopic organisms or bacteria and viruses and parasites, which even though you don't see, yet if they enter your body they can make you sick, you'll be labeled a lunatic who deserved to die at the stakes. That's because microbes could not be seen then and now with the unaided eye. Today, by the reason of equipment such as the electron microscope, the microbial world, unseen to the naked eye, may be seen. Understand therefore that because you do not see it, does not mean it does not exist. Also, because you do not hear it or feel it, does not mean it is not there. As you are reading this, believe it or not, a spirit may be whispering to you. Just because you are not in tuned to it or do not hear it, does not mean it's not going on. For example, there are certain animals that can hear sounds or see things that human beings cannot hear or see. It does not mean that fire crackers and rockets and arrows are not being released in the spirit world. It all depends on what you and I are able to perceive. 1 Kings 22: 2. An idea came to Ahab, the king of Israel. He may not have thought about it before but when King Jehoshaphat his in-law, from the section of the country called Judah, came to visit him. Then an idea just came into his mind that 'Ramoth Gilead belongs to us, don't you think we should go and take it back?' Just an idea. I want you to understand that every good or evil idea originates from the mind, but the inspiration may be from a spirit. Now go to verse 19, remember he just had an idea. However, because Jehoshaphat was a man of God, he suggests that they seek the face of God to see whether the idea is in line with His will. Many of us need to do this whenever we get ideas. In verse 19, Micaiah a prophet of God said, "I saw the LORD sitting on his throne, and all the host of heaven standing by him on his right hand and on his left." You need to pray that God will open your eyes so that you can see what others cannot see. Always remember that because you do not see it, does not mean it does not exist. Micaiah saw what others did not see. Note the word 'host', it tells us there are multitudes, myriads of individuals, personalities that cannot be seen with the naked human natural eyes. He saw the "host of heaven standing" before Him.

Realize that God was seated upon a throne. In the spirit world there are thrones, authorities, powers and dominions. As we go to examine this further, you'll see that many things on earth or in the physical realm actually follow the pattern of the heavens or the spiritual realm. That is why when Moses was building the sanctuary, God told him to make it exactly after the pattern that he was shown (Ex. 25:9). God showed him the tabernacle of the sanctuary in heaven and He said to him to make the one that will be done on earth exactly after it. Your official protocol "Thy will be done on earth as it is in heaven". There are many physical things that resemble spiritual things. A lot of times when the Bible talks about heaven, it is talking about the spiritual realm or what some people term the fourth dimension. When Paul said he was taken or caught up to the third heavens, he was saying that he was caught up to the spiritual realm, to the realm of the unseen. May God open your eyes henceforth so that you may see what others cannot see and hear what they cannot hear.

The Hosts of heaven were standing by God's right and left hand; understand that good hosts and evil hosts exist. It is not exactly a classification that those on the right or left are good and bad respectively. Rather, the differentiation is meant to help us understand that there is a division that some are good and some are evil. Nonetheless, they are all subject to God's authority. They all come under the dominion of the Most High. In the book of Job Chapter 1, the Bible reveals that at a certain day, all the Sons of God came together to meet with God. I call it the 'Board meeting of Heaven'. So periodically, there is a board meeting whereby there are discussions and deliberations; 'what shall we do now, who shall we send, how shall we treat this particular case?' Each one of them will begin to bring a case whereby a person, family, a ministry or a country is deliberated upon; the spirits begin to make suggestions. The Bible says in Job 1:6 that when the board meeting was taking place, Satan also presented himself. Satan, the wicked, evil, deceiving serpent was also there. The Bible reveals that both good and bad spirits exist nonetheless; they are all subject to the Most High. In

1st Kings 22:20 God requested of the surrounding hosts "who will?" That is where the idea came from. Ahab just had an idea not knowing that the idea came from the spirit world. Many times when you have an idea, you should check it out to make sure that it's in line with the will of God because sometimes demons may speak in order to confuse you or make you fall eventually. It may look good, but the end of it may be destruction. God asked who will go and persuade Ahab so that he will go to Ramoth and fall there. Different spirits came forward giving one suggestion or the other, [verse 21-22]. Guess what? The Lord blessed the suggestion of a lying/seducing spirit. God said in verse 22, "you shall persuade him, and also prevail...go out and do so". The spirit only gave a suggestion and God loved the idea so He blessed the spirit to prosper as he carries forth the plan.

In 1st Chronicles 21: 1, there is the nation of Israel that God had established but Satan wanted to nullify the purpose and the plan of God. The bible says Satan now stood against Israel seeking whom to use, and what to do in order to bring a set back into the plan of God for the nation, it's people, families, ministries or individuals. So Satan looks for whom to use, a person who is willing, who is in a position of authority and who is ready to subject himself for his use. Once he finds the right person, he also drops 'an idea' into the mind of the unsuspecting. Satan went to David and gave him an idea to number Israel reasoning that "how could David rule a nation and not know how many they were." But God had previously commanded that a complete census of Israel should not be done, because they shall be like the sand of the seas. He said anybody below 20 years of age should not be numbered. David was a man of scripture. He knew not to do it but because of momentary pride, he thought the idea to be a good one and he went against the will and purpose of God. 'An idea;' I pray that an evil idea will not drop into your mind in Jesus name. Better yet, I pray that you will not act upon an evil idea that is dropped into your mind in Jesus name. We cannot stop ideas; they will come. You might just be looking at someone and think wow, I like this man/lady; maybe I can invite him/her out. It's an idea, and you begin to work on it. Such ideas will not come to your minds in the name of Jesus. In verse 14 a plague was released upon the land as a form of punishment for David's willful disobedience. Just one angel administered a plague that killed seventy thousand people. Again I emphasize to you that the spirit world controls a lot of events that happen in the natural. That is why our actions and decisions may be motivated by the activity of the spirit world around our lives. Things do not just happen; there is usually a puppet master behind the scene. One angel of the Lord was able to administer a plague and kill thousands of people. Believe it or not, many plagues that suddenly spring up nowadays are being administered by angels.

Characteristics of the Spirit World

It's a real environment, with innumerable beings of all shapes and sizes with different abilities and strength. They have been in existence before the physical world (Daniel 7:9-10). Where ever there are thrones, they are dominion, authority, power, servants, and rulers. There are activities going on that most people are unaware of. Yet these activities affect most of what goes on in the physical.

There is a spiritual language. For there to be organization and order, there must be communication. Where there's lack of communication, there's chaos, and disorganization. Thus spirits have a means of communication. They have their own spoken language and believe it not, they understand all earthly languages. We cannot understand them unless we have been given the grace, usually for a limited time. It is important and imperative for most if not all believers, to receive the ability to speak in tongues. It enhances our communication with the spirit world. The Bible says, "he that speaks in tongues does not speak to man," because man cannot understand him. If you do not know how to speak in tongues, I pray the Holy Spirit will come upon you and enable you to do so. Once you begin, you are communicating with heaven. There is a language of the spirit that the average man cannot understand. In 2nd Corinthians 12: 4 Paul heard words that he couldn't understand, "inexpressible words". He knew that they were speaking and saying something but he could not understand. Unless you are given discernment or interpretation, it will not make sense to you. This should not stop you from believing that there is communication in the heavens.

As was earlier said, the spirit world is made up of good and evil spirits, and there is a good and evil kingdom. Between the two there is constant war, and God has permitted it that way for a time. Within the kingdoms there is hierarchy. Every kingdom has a hierarchy and a set of rules, regulations, laws, and principles by which it operates. Both the kingdom of good and the kingdom of evil have it. To understand that these two kingdoms are in opposition, refer to the book of Daniel where he prayed to God and God sent the angel Gabriel to deliver Daniel's request. Another angel called the prince of Persia, which God did not send, came to resist and oppose the good angel Gabriel that was bringing the blessing to Daniel. God did not send the wicked prince of Persia, but there is a system of intelligence and espionage in the spirit realm that is much more advance and sophisticated than what is known in the physical realm. This example proves that evil angels do not always need permission from God before they interfere in the affairs of man. I want to believe that the times they seek permission from God, such as in the case of Job (Job. 1:6-9), is when they have attempted havoc against a child of God and failed. Then the demonic world would petition God to remove the hedge of protection surrounding His child. Satan also petitioned Jesus for the destruction of Peter (Luke 22:31). If Jesus had not told Peter, he would not have known that he was on satan's hit list. Now imagine how many unsuspecting people live day by day under satan's radar. The more you and I align with God, the less advantage satan's host would take of us. The Bible warns us not to be ignorant of the devices of the devil so that he does not take an advantage over us (2 Cor. 2:11). Even though God knows and can stop satanic activities, but by principle, the entire human race is in a battle. Unless we continually commit ourselves to God, we cannot effectively resist satanic activities against one person, a family, or even a ministry or community.

The satanic kingdom is made up of hierarchy. This demonic kingdom is made up of rulers, powers, principalities and all types of wicked spirits in the air (Ephesians 6:12). These wicked spirits are generally called demons or devils. For the sake of differentiation, grass root or messenger evil spirits are demons while evil angels are those spirits that were cast out of heaven with satan (Rev. 12:9). Evil angels are the real devils. Demons are not angels. Devils are part of the angelic hosts, spiritual wickedness, in high authority. Angels can transfigure themselves to take the appearance of a human but they cannot embody a person. Demons can enter the bodies of humans, animals, plants and trees and non-living things. They mostly seek to manifest their character through human medium. Most people have a hard time dealing with demon spirits, how much more dealing with evil angels. According to the Bible, any angel that changes it's "estate" (structural characteristics) are put into everlasting chains and bondage (Jude 1:6); some are there right now. Angels cannot embody a person, but demons can because they have no bodies of their own. Genesis 6 explains how demons came to be; angels came from above and began to copulate with mankind. They took as many women as possible and had children by them. The children they gave birth to were called nephinims. They were giant, unusual, half human, and half devil hybrid. These hybrid human giants became disemvbodied when the Lord sent the flood during the days of Noah. However, the disembodied spirits were eternal and wicked. They continued to live till today and their primary purpose is to possess human and sometimes animal bodies. This theory is what is believed to be the origin of demon. Another theology teaches that certain angels have the ability to multiply. Scripture however does not support this. The Bible lays emphasis that angels do not marry neither are they given in marriage; they do not conceive or give birth. They need a human channel and that is why they copulated with human females in order to pollute the human race and multiply their personality.

The important fact is that demon spirits are the ones that possess human beings. In Luke 8, as discussed earlier, the Bible highlights the man of Gadara. He was possessed having legions (at least 6,000) of spirits which had a leader. That is why at times, they say "I" or "we" are many. Because the demon spirits possessed him, the Bible says he had supernatural strength to break every chain that was used to tie him down. He had no shame, he was naked. He was not afraid of anything thing so he lived in the tombs, among the dead. Legion met his match when he met Jesus. Mary Magdalene had seven spirits cast out of her. In Acts 16, there was a young girl with the spirit of divination. By the indwelling presence of this spirit the young girl was able to foretell events that would happen. Once the spirit was cast out by Paul, the girl became normal. Demons can also possess houses or buildings causing them to be haunted as earlier stated. A few years ago in Dublin, I stayed as a guest in a house that was haunted. The occupants of the house were Christians. The demon spirit would come almost nightly and harass them. Twice during my four day visit I was awaken about 2am with palpitation and sweat all over. During the second encounter, The Holy Spirit enabled me to see into the spirit realm and I saw a huge dark vapor drifting through my room and out the window. I could see the distinction between the head of the demon and the rest of the body. This revelation along with my host's testimony of how the spirit had followed them from where they previously lived confirmed to me that the house was possessed and haunted. This demon had been harassing them for over two years. My last night in the house was used to vigil and to anoint the entire house especially the doors and windows. The sweet family that hosted me have not heard from that demon since. Jesus gave us power to trample upon serpents and scorpions and over all the powers of the enemy (Luke 10:19). Halleluyah.

There are limited attacks that can come against you from the outside if you are standing firm in Christ. What these evil spirits try to do then, is to attack from the inside. God's Angels can only defend you exteriorly. The Bible says that the angels of the Lord encamp around them that fear Him and delivers them, and that angels are ministering spirits to the heirs of salvation. Angels will guide against accidents, "dashing our foot against the stone" (Psalm 91:12), arrows that are flying and external harms if we're dwelling under God's shadow. They however can hardly do anything with whatever you allow into yourself. Remember, your thoughts and ideas motivate your actions (Mark 7:15). So if you allow evil to come inside you, angels cannot interfere. That is why we need the Holy Ghost and the Word of God.

The kingdom of God is only made up of angels. There are no demons permanently dwelling there; we only have God whom the Bible calls the Father of spirits. Then we have angels that exist to worship and serve God and protect us. Understand that if there is a spirit world with constant activities going on, there are factors that will attract good or evil spirits to you. These are the door ways previously discussed. First is the way you use your senses. If you use our senses to listen, view, or do wrong things, you're inviting demon spirits. They are looking for ways to express themselves so when they see somebody that loves to listen to certain types of music, or watch certain types of movies, they would want to inhabit that person so that they can express themselves through that individual. The Bible says in Hebrews 5:14 that spiritual maturity is very important. If you are spiritually mature, you will be able to call your senses back when they go astray or go haywire. You will be able to purge your mind with the blood of Jesus. Failure to do so fills your mind with earthly garbage, which demon spirits will take advantage of. In Genesis 4 when God was having a conversation with Cain, God knew what was going on in Cain's mind. God said "Cain, you are angry," anger is not initially from the devil, it is an emotion. God gave Cain a warning to beware of what he was about to do because **"sin lies at the door"**. That is, there were demon spirits waiting to work on his emotions and sin was personalized there to mean a spirit. Demon spirits wait to play on your emotions, to move or motivate you to do what you're not supposed to do. The way you use your senses or emotions attract demons or God's angels. Another way is by certain practices such as yoga and hypnosis. A lot of people like to purge and free their minds through relaxation therapies. You must be very careful about this because if you are not under the blood, you are calling demon spirits into you by these mediums. When demons see an open door, they run through it. Keep in mind that there are many of them, all over the world. Another way to attract demons is by certain repetitions of words or phrases. In some religions or cults, people must say certain things a number of times, and some of these invite and welcome demon spirits. The mystical "Six and Seven Books of Moses" contain this methodology. Some people have gotten to the act whereby they know certain names of angels that they call up, and when they are called in a ritualistic manner, they answer. Music, drums, or instruments also thrills and attract demon spirits. Sacrifices that involve the shedding of blood are another important factor that attracts these spirits because they thirst and hunger for blood. Deuteronomy 35:33 says that whenever blood is shed upon a nation, the land becomes defiled, and there is nothing that can cause atonement unless the blood of the person who shed the blood is also spilled. Covenant is another factor. A simple promise to a friend or lover is spiritually binding. Failure to fulfill your word will attract judgment. Many cult members have release the names of family members as a covenant. These individuals without knowing may have their lives interrupted by demonic activities in the same way that God is involved in the life of any baby that is dedicated to Him by covenant.

So you see, the spirit world is very real and complicated. The primary way that you know what's going on in the spirit realm around you is by the dreams you have. If in his or her right mind, a candidate of deliverance should always be asked to tell the types of dreams he or she has been having. Noting especially the recent dreams or the dreams often repeated. Anyone who does not remember his dreams is covered with a spiritual blindfold so that he will not discern danger and consequently will be unable to prevent its occurrence. Dreams that may indicate obsession include driving or walking around aimlessly as if lost. Dreams that may indicate suppression include the sensation of paralysis while asleep, physical combat between you and one or more individuals, dwelling in an enclosed place with limited space for movement. Dreams that may indicate oppression include you running from opposition or battle or identities such as masquerades, appearing much younger than your current age, sitting for and failing exams or attending a junior class then you currently are in. Dreams that indicate possession may include eating cooked and uncooked food, being forced or seduced to have sex with someone you may or may not know, seeing someone you know by instinct but who has a more evil appearance. Eating uncooked flesh especially with blood is a definite sign of initiation into the occults or witchcraft. It is a covenant ritual. You should engage in serious prayers if you have had such an experience. Regardless, you should always pray when you have strange dreams. As you wake up the countenance of your spirit man would give you the first hint to the meaning of the dream, even if you cannot not fully understand or remember. Talk to your Pastor (who should be a trusted man of God) and ask him to interpret the dream and pray against any demonic message it may carry. Now let's consider specific types of dreams for better understanding.

Activity and Desire Dreams: People who are busy bodies and gossips may have dreams based on their life style. People who like to eat may also have persistent dreams whereby they are constantly eating. If you like to party, hang out in clubs or if you are a drug or sex addict, it is quite likely that you will dream conforming dreams.

> **For a dream comes through much activity,**
> **And a fool's voice *is known* by *his* many words.**
>
> **Ecclesiastes 5:3**

> **It shall even be as when a hungry man dreams,**
> **And look—he eats;**
> **But he awakes, and his soul is still empty;**
> **Or as when a thirsty man dreams,**
> **And look—he drinks;**

> But he awakes, and indeed *he is* faint,
> And his soul still craves:
> So the multitude of all the nations shall be,
> Who fight against Mount Zion."

Isaiah 29:8

You will see yourself in dreams engaged in your desires and activities regularly. Very often, what you do and what you desire are reflected in your dream life. Such dreams are not messages from God or the spirit world but are the conversion of your natural habitual feeling and behavior into your subconscious. These dreams do not make you spiritual but strengthens your carnal nature. Note that scripture says that when you wake up "your soul still craves". The remedy is for you to allow the word of God to cleans you and transform you by the renewal of your mind. Make this confession right now three times, "I have the mind of God". I sanitize every filthiness of your flesh and spirit with the blood of Jesus. No longer shall your dreams be dictated by the activities and desires of your flesh, but by the spirit of God in Jesus name.

Warning and Revelation Dreams: Genesis chapter 41 narrates the story of Pharaoh's dream interpreted by Joseph to mean seven prosperous years followed by seven years of severe famine. The dream was given to Pharaoh twice in different forms. The symbol in one was grain and the symbol in the other was cattle but the interpretation for both dreams was the same. When God sends a warning to you, it is not unusual for the dream to be repeated more than once and in different forms. But the interpretation will be the same. It is also not unusual for God to give revelations to heathens and unbelievers, especially if they are authority figures in the context of the message. They can be head of a household, head of an enterprise of a nation. God will always honor their position. They may not know the interpretation, but God will nevertheless give them the message. They are now responsible, if they are wise to seek for the meaning. Daniel chapter four informs that a similar event occurred in the life of Nebuchadnezzar, the king of Babylon. He was given an important revelation, forgot if and then held at ransom the wise men and sorcerers of his kingdom until someone could tell him the exact dream and its interpretation. Only an act of God through Daniel and his friends gave the king his heart's desire. Every dream from God has a meaning and an interpretation. If you do not understand the message of the dream or vision, you should be willing to pray until you obtain the interpretation. Otherwise you may take a shortcut and seek someone who has the gift of interpretation of revelations or who is a seer. I always caution those who go about seeking interpreters, prophets and seers for solution. You need to discernment of their calling and motive. Not all interpretations require the operation of the Holy Spirit. Many who practice witchcraft and sorcery may be gifted so see and interpret your revelation. If they receive a revelation about you or if you relate your dreams to them, they may use it against you. Remember Balaam used what he saw concerning the Israelites against them by telling Balak to seduce the Israelite men with the Moab women and cause God's people to commit whoredom and idolatry (Numbers 25:1-13).

Joseph was given a revelation dream when he was a teenager (Genesis 37:5-10). This dream foretold the plan and purpose of God for his life. It was prophetic. These types of dreams are usually for preparation and edification. On the one hand they are meant to keep you focused so you will not get frustrated by hardship, distracted by the temporal or complacent by satisfaction of the inferior before reaching the goal. On the other hand, revelation dreams are meant to keep you submission to the will of God without faltering, should the experience be unsavory. Jesus revealed to Peter what type of death he would die to glorify Him (John 21:15-19). Peter accepted this as Jesus accepted the purpose of God for Him to die for humanity. It is always good to pray whenever you receive a revelation that does not portray a good message. Jesus prayed that the cup of death would be removed because of the devastation He would have to go through. He concluded His prayer at all times by saying, "not as I will, but Your will be done". If you don't like the message of a revelation you receive, ask that God would let the cup pass over you, but the bottom line is that His will be done in your life to the glory of His name. Sometimes revelation dreams have to do with coming events based on God's judgment which will not be altered. Genesis chapter 40 narrates the judgment of the Pharaoh's butler and baker. Each had a dream which gave a revelation of what would happen to them. It happened just as Joseph had interpreted. Be conscious of the revelation and warning dreams that you have. As a child of God, His Spirit will warn you if you are in a wrong relationship or if something bad is about to happen to you or a loved one. God may even give you a message of warning for others in your household or your Church. Everyone in authority has the right to receive messages for those who are under them. God honors position. Thus a parent should receive revelation about their children and spiritual leaders should receive revelations about those who submit to them. Jesus was able to warn Peter of satan's plan to destroy him (Luke 22:31-32) because of the relationship they had. More will be taught on the results of association later in this book under the section of Soul ties.

Instructional Dreams: Many times revelation and warning dreams contain instructions for the one who is given the revelation. In Matthew 2:13, an angel in a dream warned Joseph the husband of Mary that king Herod was after the life of the infant Jesus to kill him. Joseph was then instructed to flee with Mary and Jesus to Egypt until he is given another instructional dream. Joseph obeyed. He did not argue, he did not complain or doubt, he simple did as he was instructed. You may be one of those Christian who when given an instruction to flee would find other scriptures to defend your position. Consider the following. Jesus was God incarnate. God's only begotten Son, surrounded constantly by angels, nevertheless, God instructed his earthly father to flee with the child and His mother because of the enemy. Instead of fleeing, some of you will begin to quote, "no weapon fashioned against me will prosper", "I am more than a conquerer through Christ Who strengthens me", and so on. You want to play superman instead of simply obeying. May God help us in Jesus name. This was the error of righteous King Josiah who began to reign when he was eight years old (2 Chronicles 35:20-24). After doing exploits for the Lord and restoring the nation worship of Jehovah, Josiah went out to battle against Necho the king of Egypt, who was in battle with another king. It was not Josiah's war and he was warned to stay out of the battle but he did not listen. Unfortunately, he was killed in a battle that had nothing to do with him-because he refused the warning to back down. Always take spiritual warnings seriously. Don't let your pride or spirituality get the best of you. If you are warned not to travel, then don't travel. If you are warned not to marry a particular person, don't marry the person. No matter how much embarrassment it will cause at that point in time. Only God knows the end from the beginning. Listen to Him.

In Acts chapter ten from verses ten to sixteen, the Apostle Peter had a vision which revealed the plan of God and the instruction for him to take the gospel to the gentiles. Because he did not fully understand the vision, since the message seemed to contradict his understanding of the will of God, he was reluctant to obey the instruction. Peter's experience clearly illustrates that your level of understanding of God will determine your level of operation in the things of God. Whenever you do not have a full understanding of a revelation, you are obligated to prayer seek the accurate meaning.

Heavenly Dreams: It is a blessing to be caught up to the third heaven (2 Corinthians 12:1-4), the very abode of the glorious God and catch a glimpse of holy angels, and other forms of divine personalities. I have been given the grace to see different types of angels over the years in dreams. I've seen a gigantic angel stand before me carrying a sword and a shield. Another time I was in the midst of several singing angels. Their music was truly out of this world. Unfortunately when I woke up, I remembered the lyric but could not remember the tune or rhythm. On an occasion I was in the presence of the glory of God and I heard Him speak to you personally. Jesus has appeared to me on a few occasions in dreams to encourage or give me instructions. I have been privileged to have other strange experiences that some of you reading this book would not believe. As Apostle Paul said, these revelations are not given for us to boast but for us to be humble and appreciative of God more than others. If you've never had heavenly dream, I pray that God would give you the grace to see a vision of heaven before you die. Your earthly perspective will undoubtedly change.

Demonic Dreams: These are dreams that reveal the operation and activities of demons against you. You will see demons in form of people, animals, insects or in their true ugly form and may be involved in battles against them where arsenals that resemble military weapons are utilized. You will feel them try to suppress and overpower you, steal money from you, cause accidents or you may experience sexual interaction with them. Some people have reported that as they dream of demonic sexual encounters their clothes are actual removed and they are strip naked and are covered with body fluids around their private parts upon waking up. This level of demonic activity is empowered by covenants and sacrifices that you may not even be aware of. There is no limit to the operation of demons in the life a person devoid of divine protection. Thank God for the empowerment of the Holy Spirit and the covering of the Blood of Jesus for the believer. Unbelievers do not have this right or benefit. Nevertheless, many believers do experience a measure of demonic dreams because of the life they had lived or the things they or their ancestors had done prior to conversion. If you were a sexual pervert before conversion, if you or your ancestor had shed innocent blood or have worshipped idols passionately prior to accepting Christ, you need to undergo deliverance. Because you are reading this book, I pray that God will hit you with an anointing for deliverance in the name of Jesus. Right now, I speak deliverance into your life. Be delivered from every demonic dream and the evil message being transmitted in Jesus name.

Chapter Six

Curses

A good understanding of the impact of curses may keep you from entanglement. Curses are not mystical and fictional. Curses are real and may be simple or complex. A curse is a spiritual invocation intended to produce harm or punishment. It is an evil or misfortune that occurs as if in response to imprecation or retribution. The invocation is usually verbal but may also involve the use of physical items such as mirrors, dolls, dirt, clothing, animal or human body parts that have spiritual significance. The target of the curse may be an individual, a group of people, including families and communities and even a race or a nation. For example, in the Bible, Balaam sought to curse the congregation of Israel by the use of divination and enchantment. Curses may also be verbalized as "prayers and confessions" by a group of persons or by someone in authority or who has been unjustly treated. Simply said, curses are penalties for disobedience or wrong doing and may be transferable, even across generations. If the reward for obedience is the blessing, it is obvious that the curse being the direct opposite of the blessing, is the reward for disobedience. Anyone who is blessed is not under a curse and anyone who is cursed is not blessed. You cannot be cursed and blessed simultaneously. Unfortunately, because you are blessed today does not guarantee you will not be cursed tomorrow if care is not taken. It will therefore be of great benef if I first give you some revelations on the blessing before expounding to you the reality and effect of curses.

In the very beginning, the Creator blessed His creation. The first reference to the blessing in scripture is found in Genesis chapter one and verse twenty-eight. This single verse reveals the purpose and power of the blessing. The blessing is not only financial as many believe. The blessing has the power to change any area of your life that is functioning below the set standard of God. After the flood the wiped out nearly all of humanity, in Genesis 9:1, the Lord blessed Noah and his sons. In Genesis 24:1, it states that "God blessed Abraham in all things". This is beyond financial satisfaction. Abraham had a total of eight children, good health, long life, large number of people who worked for and served him. Simply put, he was great in his generation because of the blessing of God. He was singled out to showcase the glory of God. I pray that God will show case you and single you out for honor in your generation. In the book of Job chapter one, Job was described as a man who was perfect and upright, who fear God and eschewed evil. For this, God blessed him and decorated his life with a beautiful family, a successful business, wealth, health, and honor in the community. Joseph (Gen. 41: 39-46), Phinehas, son of Eleazar the priest (Num. 25: 11-12), David (2 Sam. 7:5-29), Solomon (1 King 3:3-14), Daniel (Dan. 2:48), Joseph of Arimathea (Matt. 27:57), Barnabas, the son of consolation (Acts 4:36-37), and many others within the pages of scripture. The multitude of testimony concerning those who were blessed within the pages of scripture provides assurance that God is a good God and that He delights in the prosperity of those who serve Him faithfully (Ps. 35:27). From the beginning, the Lord had been a God of blessing.

> *Then God blessed them, and said to them, "Be fruitful and multiply;*
> *Fill the earth and subdue it; have dominion over the fish of the sea,*

> *Over the birds of the air, and over every living thing*
> *that moves on*
> *The earth."*

Gen. 1:28

The blessing is an impartation as also the curse is an impartation. It is an authoritative command released into your life. In technical terminology, it is the programing of your life to function at the optimum level. In a similar way, the curse can be authoritatively release into the life of the disobedient to function below standard.

By principle, the lesser is blessed by the greater (Hebrews 7:7), because you cannot give what you don't have. Let us examine in detail the ingredients that make up the blessing and corresponding curses. There are five dimensions to the blessing.

"Be fruitful": Means to increase and not be barren. Fruitfulness always requires a viable seed, because there cannot be a fruit without a seed. The initial seed you use to bear fruit is given to you by God. "God gives seed to the sower" (Isaiah 55:10). This is the output of grace lest any man should boast. A direct curse against this dimension of blessing is the curse of barrenness or childlessness, lack and failure to thrive. Oppressive demons operate in this dimension. The devourer demon is empowered because of a curse to destroy your harvest and keep you from prospering. Malachi 3:9 declares that everyone who robs God of tithes and offerings are "cursed with a curse". Pretty graphic language. Disobedience to the ordinance of God regarding tithes and offering initiates a curse in your life which empowers the demon spirit to operate. Curses are usually enforced by demons and evil angels while blessings are enforced by holy angels. I relieve of their duties every demon assigned to punish you in Jesus name. As you believe in this writing, the angels of God will reposition to bless you. Goodness and mercy shall follow you henceforth in the mighty name of Jesus.

"Multiply": Means to be enlarged and to expand. To have great potential and far reaching influence. Genesis 28:14 states that, "Also your descendants shall be as the dust of the earth; you shall spread abroad to the west and the east, to the north and the south; and in you and in your seed all the families of the earth shall be blest'. To multiply it is the outcome of fruitfulness. Curse against your ability to multiple is termed the curse of limitation. Suppressive demons operate in this dimension. God placed a curse of limitation upon the household of Eli because he honored his sons more than God and despite many warnings from God, Eli did not rebuke his sons for their corruption and perversion. God renounced the priesthood from the household of Eli and said none would grow to be old and many would live with sickness (1 Samuel 2:29-34). God placed a curse of limitation on their health, success/achievement and age. If you are under such a curse, today I declare you to be released in the name of Jesus. Go multiply and spread abroad.

"Replenish": Means to refill, replace or to restore. This dimension of the blessing guarantees the constant replenishment of depleted resources so that there is no end to the goodness of God in your life. In terms of restoration, it guarantees the replacement of resources that were either, stolen by the enemy (Job being a perfect example), given away or lost by the owner. In summary, this dimension of the blessing is what empowers the following laws;

i.   The Lord is my Shepherd, I shall not lack (Psalm 23:1, 34:10).

Blessed shall be your basket and your store (Deut 28:5).

ii. A thief who is caught must restore one to four folds of what he has stolen (Exodus 22:1-4). A prayer point against spiritual thieves, including the devil himself is to command them to return four folds of what they have stolen from you. Zacchaeus put this principle to practice when he met with Jesus (Luke 19:8). God also promised to restore the years that the locust, the caterpillar and all other forms of devouring powers have eaten away in your life (Joel 2:25). This is a great blessing. When you give, you are guaranteed a return, giving to others becomes an investment that yields dividend (Luke 6:38).

The curse that opposes replenishment will make you a continuous beggar and borrower, instead of being a giver and a lender. You will not be able to save money or accumulate any good thing because the power to replenish, save up and be restored has been cancelled in your life. As you are reading these words I reverse every curse against your ability to replenish. Because Jehovah has favored you (in His favor is life) you shall have abundant life in Jesus name.

"Subdue": Means to overpower, overtake, overcome, prevail and succeed. This dimension of the blessing is for victory and protection against evil. You will be above only and never beneath (Deuteronomy 28:13). You are empowered to be a winner in competition, victorious in battle and successful in endeavor. Life is full of challenges. You have to jump one huddle after the other. In order not to live in defeat, you need to experience this blessing. This dimension of the blessing also keeps you healthy and provides healing when you are sick. Your body is made up of an immune system that attacks and destroys foreign intruders called antigens. These intruders are kept in check or subdued by your body's immune system.

The curse that opposes your ability to subdue will cause you to fail where most succeed, allow the enemies to overcome you and sickness, especially sickness that are not easily cured, to prevail. The results of this curse can be summarized in the following passages;

> ***The LORD will send on you cursing, confusion and rebuke***
> ***In all that you set your hands to do, until you are destroyed***
> ***And until you perish quickly, because of the wickedness of your doings in which you have forsaken Me.***

The LORD will make the plague to cling to you until He has
Consumed you.....
The LORD will strike you with consumption, with fever, with
Inflammation, with severe burning fever, with the sword, with
With scorching, and with mildew. They shall pursue you until
You perish.
The LORD will strike you with the boils of Egypt, with tumors (cancer), with the scab, and with the itch (hypersensitivity and allergy) from
Which you cannot be healed.
The LORD will strike you with madness (psychosis), and blindness and confusion of heart (emotional distress).
And you shall grope at noon day as a blind man gropes in darkness
You shall not prosper in your ways. You shall be only oppressed and plundered continually, and no one shall save you.

Deuteronomy 28: 20-22, 27-29
(Parenthesis mine)

May the Lord grant you deliverance from the curse of the law causing sickness and defeat in your life in Jesus name. I destroy the power of every stranger buying and selling in your life as well as the operation of every oppressive spirit against you in the name above every other name.

"Have Dominion": Means to be in control, to rule and have authority over, to be at peace, confident and without fear. This is the outcome of being able to "subdue" opposition in the same manner as "multiply" is the outcome of "fruitfulness". This is the greatest dimension of the blessing. It reveals the essence of man on earth, the real reason why God created mankind. God made man in His image and likeness (Genesis 1:26-28) to represent Him on earth in all affairs. Man was to know the mind of God, speak and exercise judgment with authority as a god over all of God's earthly creation (Psalms 82:6). Psalms eight and verses five and six declares, "You made him a little lower than angels and have crowned him with glory and honor. You made him to have dominion over the works of Your hands. You put all things under his feet". Man was created to dominate, not be dominated. "Don't you know that we shall judge angels? How much more things that pertains to this life" (1 Corinthians 6:3). When man is in one accord with God he is blessed to dominate, but when he rebels against God his position is inverted and he is dominated. He no longer is in control but is under the control of other agents, spirits and forces. He is not even able to control his own thoughts and actions. Before the fall man had the authority to rule over the activities of angels and demons on the earth. Eve had authority of the speaking, crafty serpent in the garden of Eden, but she did not use her authority. Instead, she yielded her will to its suggestion. After the fall this authority was suppressed and man was ruled by his instinct, lust and imagination. He went from being on top to being beneath and the desire of his heart was geared towards evil continually. He was under the influence of the fallen flesh and the fallen spirits. Re-positioning back to his rightful place of authority can only be exercised by faith in the name of Jesus, the Restorer and Redeemer. Only in His name shall every knee bow and every tongue confess to His Lordship. It is therefore by reason of this dimension of the blessing that you are empowered by the Holy Ghost to function as a king, a priest or a prophet.

The curse that opposes your ability to dominate keeps your heart darkened and blind to the Gospel. You subject yourself to this curse when you deliberately resist the faith and you oppose those who have accepted the faith. You refuse to acknowledge God for selfish reasons even though you have a conviction of His existence. This curse will bring you to shame and destroy you physically as well as spiritually.

It is the final stage of complete enslavement. You live a shameful life and then when you die, you're hell bound. The following scripture summarizes the impact of the curse that keeps you from reigning as a king, a priest or a prophet.

> *Because that, when they knew God, they did not glorify Him as*
> *God, neither were thankful, but became vain in their imaginations,*
> *And their foolish hearts were darkened. Professing to be wise, they became fools. And changed the glory of the incorruptible God into an image made like corruptible man, and to birds, four footed beasts and creeping things. Therefore God also gave them up to uncleanness through the lust of their own hearts, to dishonor their bodies between themselves. Who changed the truth of God into a lie, who worship and serve the creature more than the Creator, Who is blest forever more. Amen.*

> *Because of this, God gave them over to shameful lusts. Even their women exchanged natural sexual relations for unnatural ones. In the same way the men also abandoned natural relations with women and were inflamed with lust for one another. Men committed shameful acts with other men, and received in themselves the due penalty for their error.*

> *Furthermore, just as they did not think it worthwhile to retain the knowledge of God, so God gave them over to a depraved mind, so that they do what ought not to be done. They have become filled with every kind of wickedness, evil, greed and depravity. They are full of envy, murder, strife, deceit and malice. They are gossips, slanderers, God-haters, insolent, arrogant and boastful; they invent ways of doing evil; they disobey their parent, they have no understanding, no fidelity,*

no love, no mercy. Although they know God's righteous decree that those who do such things deserve death, they not only continue to do these very things but also approve of those who practice them.

Romans 1:21-3

The above passage reveals that a curse is the consequence of rebelling against the true God. It also reveals that the origin of every curse is as a result of dishonor to God. You should understand that most people who engage in shameful and uncontrollable unrighteous behaviors are cursed. Because they are unable to stop these shameful behaviors, they now seek for excuses or evidences to support their shame and make it appear as the norm so the majority would accept or tolerate them. For example, everything in nature bears witness that it is abnormal for mankind to have sex with animals, yet some do. How many documented research do we have of female animals flirting or having sex with each other, yet some human females have such a lifestyle. Neither do we see male animals flirting or having sex with each other. But some humans do. Some people feel so uncomfortable with their gender that they have undergone gender operations to change. Others who cannot change their genders live out their lives pretending to be the opposite sex. The universal agenda of the gay, lesbian, bisexual and transgender (GLBT) community is to play on every one's intelligence by making you believe that an abnormal behavior is normal. It's not normal, it's a curse. According to the passage above, "they've become vain in their imaginations and their foolish hearts have become darkened". This is the effect of the curse. The curse can distort your perception of reality in order to destroy you. Homosexuality is a psychological disorder just as schizophrenia, bipolar and multi-personality disorders. Instead of seeking justification, they should seek treatment. Many have become homosexuals because they were lured or force into the behavior by friends or family members. And now there is a psychological agenda in the so called developed world to brainwash the rest of humanity into accepting this perversion as the norm. This agenda is channeled through the educational system and is powered by political legislature in many countries because those who seat in power are either homosexuals or have family members who are homosexuals. I don't believe that any one was born homosexual, unless they were born with some measure of mental deficiency. I believe that some people are born with a tendency towards increase gender expression by reason of a female being prone to more masculine behavior or a male being prone to more feminine behavior. For example, some females can have deep voices, muscular build and athletic, or have domineering attitudes. This does not equate them to be a man. Gender differentiation is for the purpose of complementation and procreation. Homosexuality is a deliberate distortion of this purpose. It is therefore a condition learnt behavior by experimentation which later becomes an addiction. I appeal in love to any open-minded homosexual to seek for deliverance. God loves you regardless and He desires to set you free. Contact me if you don't know the next step to take. Give Jesus a chance to change your heart.

There are a growing number of GLBT attending Church. As with politics, some are being ordained as ministers. This is a great error. Of course, everyone has the right to go to Church. Jesus declared, "Come unto me all you that labor and are heavy laden, I will give you rest (Matthew 11:28). So, whether you're a thief, a prostitute, a corrupt politician, a homosexual, name it. For all have sinned and come short of the glory of God. Without Christ, we are all hell bound anyway. We come to Church to accept Christ, learn about His ways and live by Biblical principles. We should not come to Church with the notion that my way of life MUST be accepted and honored by the Church doctrine. To ordain gay ministers is equivalent to ordaining known prostitutes and sociopaths. The air force will not recruit people with known vision disorder, neither will the military enlist those with certain disabilities. It is therefore not offensive for GLBT to be excluded from officiating in the ministry of Christ, known as the universal Church. It's not about denomination any longer, it's about the Body of Christ. There's only one Body, one Spirit, one LORD, one faith and one Baptism (Ephesians 4:4-5).

The spiritual principle or rule of thumb regarding curses is that a curse has no effect if there is no cause.

> *Like a fluttering sparrow or a darting swallow, an underserved curse will not land on its intended victim. (Proverbs 26:2 NLT)*

To be precise, there are three major reasons why a curse would affect it's intended victim. A person maybe cursed based on the choices he makes, the confession of his mouth and the people he associates with. That is, your behavior can result in consequences that enhances life or death, blessing or cursing (Deut. 30:15). The words you speak or confess can impact your life or death, blessing or cursing (Prov. 18: 21) and you can also be yoked together (in agreement or in a relationship) with a person who is blessed or who is cursed (2 Cor. 6:14). By so doing, you will share in their consequences of good or evil.

Origin of Curses: Every curse has an origin or a source. The source is the agent that invokes the curse on a person, place or thing. Remember that the definition of a curse is evil or misfortune that befalls a person due to retribution or imprecation. Every offense carries a penalty which may be mild, moderate or severe. God, the sovereign Creator of the universe has ordained laws by which His universe is governed and stabilized. There are Natural laws which uphold the physical universe and Supernatural laws which uphold the spiritual universe. In between these two dimensions exists a bridge that is known as Moral laws. Simply put, the consequence of moral laws allow or disallow the passage from the physical realm into the spiritual realm.

A law is a theoretical principle deduced from facts that a particular phenomenon will always occur if certain conditions are present. We learn what is fact from experience, that is the repetition or reproducibility of an event becomes a fact (this is the basis of scientific experiments), but the eternal God, Who knows the end from the beginning, does not need to experiment. He knows the TRUTH because He is the

TRUTH. Facts are evidences which bear witness to the truth. The truth is standard and cannot be altered. Many a times, depending on the presentation of events, facts may not equate to the truth. A common example is the fact of the devastation of sickness and poverty in the world. Based on these facts many say that God is not a good God. A good God, they claim, will never allow terrible things to happen to His creation. The truth obviously is that "God is good" and He is not responsible for the stage of chaos that the world is in. God created the Earth and its inhabitant, and thereafter gave the lease over to Adam and his descendants to dominate for a set time. In the Garden of Eden Satan deceived Adam into giving him the title deed to the Earth. Satan now became the "ruler of this world" or the "god of this age (John 14:30, 2 Cor. 4:4)" for the set time it was given to Adam. God honored the transition of ownership and thus has limited His influence upon the Earth. It is therefore not God's fault that the Earth is in a chaotic state. Those who insist that God is a terrible God lack the completed fact of the matter. For those of us who know the complete fact as revealed in the holy scriptures, we are assured that God is good, because we know the Truth. When you have faith in God, you don't need to have all the facts presented to you. Faith gives you conviction of what is truth.

> **But you have an unction from the Holy One, and you know all things. I have not written you because you know not the truth, but because you know it, and that no lie is of the truth.**
>
> **1 John 2:20-21**

God told Adam the truth when he was first created and place in the Garden of Eden. Mankind was blessed because God had invoked five dimension of the blessing upon humanity through Adam. Satan, the eternal enemy of mankind understood by personal experience that the blessing can only be changed to a curse when the person who has been blest breaks the covenant of blessing through disobedience. He therefore sought for an occasion to deceive mankind into disobeying the precept of God.

> *And the L*ORD *God commanded the man, "You are free*
> *to eat from any tree in the garden, but you must not*
> *eat from the tree of the knowledge of good and evil, for*
> *when you eat from it you will certainly die."*
>
> > **Genesis 2:16-17**

Why would God grant access to the Tree of the Knowledge of Good and Evil all the while instructing Adam not to eat of it, when it would result in death if eaten? God placed a condition or test before Adam because every covenant is established based on conditions. If you adhere to the condition, you enjoy the blessing but if you default, you are punished. The punishment is the curse. God gives you a condition or a test but He does not deceive or tempt you to fail the test. Temptation is from the enemy or the lust of your flesh, not from God as James confirm (James 1:13-15), and its purpose is for you to default on the covenant. Temptation is therefore a stimulus. It is a catalyst for disobedience and failure in order for you to be punished with a cursed.

> **"You will not certainly die,"** the serpent said to the
> woman. "For God knows that when you eat from it
> your eyes will be opened, and you will be like God,
> knowing good and evil."
>
> > **Genesis 3:4-5**

Satan lied to Eve, deceiving her into disobedience. Eve disobeyed and encouraged her husband Adam to disobey God as well.

> *When the woman saw that the fruit of the tree was good*
> *for food and pleasing to the eye, and also desirable for*
> *gaining wisdom, she took some and ate it. She also gave*
> *some to her husband, who was with her, and he ate it.*
>
> > **Genesis 3:6**

Now, was it unfair for God to ask Adam and Eve not to eat of one single tree when He had given them the right to eat from hundreds of other trees? I think it's very fair of God. As a matter of fact, it is very generous of God. Unfortunately, the one tree that God instructed Adam and Eve not to eat is the one they ate, even though God told them what would happen if they ate of it. They did not eat of the Tree of Life that was also in the Garden, rather they preferred the tree they would cause them to die. God consequently responded by punishing or rather, cursing the serpent who yielded himself to be used by satan, Eve for yielding to temptation and the earth for Adam's sake. So you see that as the blessing originated from God likewise the curse originated from God as a punishment for disobedience.

So the LORD God said to the serpent, "Because you have done this,

> **"Cursed are you above all livestock**
> **and all wild animals!**
> **You will crawl on your belly**
> **and you will eat dust**
> **all the days of your life.**
>
> **And I will put enmity**
> **between you and the woman,**
> **and between your offspring and hers;**
> **he will crush your head,**
> **and you will strike his heel."**
>
> **To the woman he said,**
>
> **"I will make your pains in childbearing very severe;**
> **with painful labor you will give birth to children.**
> **Your desire will be for your husband,**
> **and he will rule over you. "**

To Adam he said, "Because you listened to your
wife and ate fruit from the tree about which I
commanded you, 'You must not eat from it,'

"Cursed is the ground because of you;
through painful toil you will eat food from it
all the days of your life.
It will produce thorns and thistles for you,
and you will eat the plants of the field.
By the sweat of your brow
you will eat your food
until you return to the ground,
since from it you were taken;
for dust you are
and to dust you will return."

Genesis 3:14-19

God directly placed a curse on the serpent and on the ground (earth), but the pronouncement on Eve and Adam was not called a curse. The blessing of God upon their lives was not annulled. It cannot be cancelled because it is the spoken word of God. It can only be limited. The blessing was made painful and more difficult to achieve. Mankind will be fruitful and they will multiple because the Lord God had spoken it, but there will be a lot of pain involved, miscarriages, and heartbreaks. Man will subdue and dominate but it would take great efforts, a lot of sweat, determination and hard work. God's word will always accomplish that for which it was sent. It may be delayed because of disobedience but it will eventually come to pass if the necessary steps are taken, as you will see shortly.

God cursed Cain because he killed his brother Abel (Genesis 4:10-15). The curse made Cain a wanderer who would be a symbol of shame to everyone who meets him to the point that someone may want to kill him. To prevent anyone from killing Cain, God placed a mark on him.

God promised to curse anyone who cursed Abram. Believers, being the off springs of Abraham by faith also benefit from this promise of God. He will curse anyone who curses you and will bless anyone who blesses you.

Everyone is entitled to be blessed or to be cursed based on the choices they make. God will bless you if you obey, but you will be cursed if you disobey. You should be aware of the fact that your choices have consequences. Some of these consequences have far reaching implications, perhaps to generations unborn.

> *"Behold, I set before you today a blessing and a curse: the blessing, if you obey the commandments of the LORD your God which I command you today: and the curse, if you do not obey the commandments of the LORD your God, but turn aside from the way which I command you today, to go after other gods which you have not known.*
>
> *Deuteronomy 11:26-28*

> *See, I have set before you today life and good, death and evil, in that I command you today to love the LORD your God, to walk in His ways, and to keep His commandments, His statutes, and His judgments, that you may live and multiply; and the LORD your God will bless you in the land which you go to possess. But if your heart turns away so that you do not hear, and are drawn away, and worship other gods and serve them, I announce to you today that you shall surely perish; you shall not prolong your days in the land which you cross over the Jordan to go in and possess. I call heaven and earth as witnesses today against you, that I have set before you life and death, blessing and cursing; <u>therefore choose life, that both you and your descendants may live;</u> that you may love the LORD your God, that you may obey His voice, and that you may*

> ***cling to Him, for He is your life and the length of your days; and that you may dwell in the land which the LORD swore to your fathers, to Abraham, Isaac, and Jacob, to give them."***

> ***Deuteronomy 30:15-20***

The reality of our lives is contained in these passages which conclude as "therefore choose life, that both you and your descendants may live". Our lives are made up of the choices we make and every choice has its consequence. Some consequences are immediate while others occur months or years after the choice has been made. This is similar to seeds that are planted. Some seeds grow and bud within weeks while others require months. In fact, you are where you are today because of the choices you made yesterday. The friends you associate with, the places you go, the car you drive, the house you live in, the Church you attend, your spouse, education and career, all these are the result of the choices you made. Whether you were inspired or deceived to make the choice does not matter. What matters most is that you made the choice and will ultimately be responsible for the consequence, be it a blessing or a curse. Every good choice you make is a blessing and every bad choice you make is a curse. Look through scripture and learn. Cain chose to be angry because his sacrifice was rejected by God but Able his brother's sacrifice was accepted. He killed his brother and was therefore cursed (Gen 4:5-13). Abram choose to obey God and leave the pagan traditions of his fathers and he and his descendants were blest (Gen. 12:1-5). Joseph chose not to yield to the temptation and seduction of his master, Potiphar's wife because he respected his master and feared God. He suffered for doing what was right but eventually he was vindicated and promoted to be ruler in the land (Gen.39-41). Jacob aided by his mother, deceived his father Isaac for the blessing of the first born, but also brought a curse upon himself in other areas of his life (Genesis 27:12). Samson chose to reveal his covenant secret to Delilah, who constantly provoked him in deception. He yielded to temptation, lost his strength and suffered at the hands of his enemies

(Judges 16: 6-19). Ruth chose to stay with her mother-in-law, Naomi after her husband die. She chose Naomi's people and God over that of the Moabites and was blest with a godly husband, Boaz and became the grandmother of Jesse, the father of David who was anointed the king of Israel (Ruth 4:13-17). David chose to fight against Goliath when everyone else were afraid and fled for their lives. He could not stand to see the uncircumcised insult the living God. He defeated Goliath and instantly rose to fame and power (1 Samuel 17:24-48). Daniel also refused to live the common perverse lifestyle of his peers but purposed in his heart to consecrate himself to his God. He was blest with wisdom and a life of success (Daniel 1). The list continues even into the New Testament. Judas, inspired by satan, chose to betray Jesus and died a tragic death (Luke 22:3, Matthew 27:2-4). John Mark chose to desert Paul and Barnabas on the mission field but his decision to join the team later was not welcomed, causing separation of holy union (Acts 13:4 &13, 15:36-41). Thousands upon hearing the gospel chose to yield to the message of salvation and follow the principles of the Holy Scriptures (Acts 2:40-45).

In Summary, keep the following in mind whenever you want to make a choose;

- A good choice becomes a blessing.

- A bad choice becomes a curse.

- Your choice affects you, those closely related to you and perhaps your coming descendants.

- Your choice is an integral part of your destiny.

It is the aspect of your destiny that you control and that allows you to receive divine acceptance or divine rejection. Your destiny is made up of two major components, what can be altered and what cannot be altered. You cannot alter your heritage at birth, parentage, gender and genetic characteristics. Some may be born poor, some are born rich. The beginning matters but should not stop you from living a fulfilled life. Job 8:7 states that "Though your beginning was small, yet your latter end would increase abundantly" and Ecclesiastes 7:8 states that "the end of a thing is better than the beginning." That which cannot be altered is governed by divine providence, divine connection, divine ordination and divine protection. But the areas of your life that can be altered is based on the choices you make. The mysterious fact is that the divine attributes are set into motion by your choices, the issues that you can change. Remember the story of Joseph. He was divinely protected from his brother's attempt to assassinate him, divine providence led him to Potiphar and divine connection introduced him to Pharaoh's butler and eventually to Pharaoh himself. He was consequently divinely ordained to a position of greatness because he continued to make good choices based on godly principles. The same will be true for your life in Jesus name.

Curses may originate from other sources as described below.

Curse from Man: A man can curse another person. In Deuteronomy 27:13, Moses selected some tribes of Israel to pronounce the curse on any one who disobeys the commandment of God for them. In Genesis 9:25 Noah cursed his grandson Canaan because Ham the father of Canaan did not cover his father's nakedness. Canaan was cursed to be a servant of servants. Noah did not curse the offender. Instead he cursed the child of the offender. Again, you see how Ham's choice to ridicule his father became a curse on his descendant. Noah was an authority figure over his household. He released a curse of limitation, slavery and servitude upon his grandson which hindered his progress and success. Even his blessed territory known as the "Land of Canaan" or the "Promise Land" was later given to another group of people called the Hebrews while the descendants of Canaan were dispossessed and many became servants hundreds of years after the curse was invoked on Canaan. Now imagine the aftermath of curses that have been rained upon children or grandchildren by their parents or grandparents. Even if you are a victim of a parental curse, be of good cheers. As you continue to read, you will receive your victory in Jesus name.

Curse from Witches and Sorcerers: Many people have been cursed through the enterprise and instrumentation of witchcraft, sorcery, potions, charms, talisman, spells, voodoo, juju, amulets, incantations etc. Witches and sorcerers are real. Many of them wear regular clothes and live in modern houses like you and me, but what they do in their spare time differs greatly from what you and I would consider leisure. These individuals are acquainted with demons and familiar spirits having acquired the knowledge of how to become mediums for demonic enterprises. Their curse could breakup families, cause sickness, accidents, lukewarm, addiction and even sin. They can bewitch an individual or a group of people. Balaam, a questionable prophet but more likely a sorcerer, was hired to curse the entire nation of Israel (Numbers 22:6-17). Simon the sorcerer, also known as Bar Jesus, had the whole city of Samaria in fear because of the power of his sorcery (Acts 8). Jezebel, the wife of king Ahab, was a renown witch, who brought the whole nation of Israel to her knees in the worship of Baal. It took the mighty prophet Elijah to begin to destroy her organized demonic religious system (1 Kg 18: 15-40). Witchcraft powers desire to invade Churches as well, if permitted. A member will join a Church and systematically weaken members by demonic activities, recruit members to themselves from among the congregation and introduce ideas or programs that will cause the Church to lose focus. They usually target Churches that are on fire for God, teaching and practicing the principles of the Holy Scriptures. Most of the time, leaders of groups, committees or the ministerial body are their target. Churches must continue steadfast in the faith, powerful prayers and scriptural doctrines. The ministry of prayer and the word of God backed up with a lifestyle of holiness must always be given priority since these are the only poison for demonic infestation.

Curse from Prophets: In another case the prophet Elisha cursed a group of youth who were making fun of him. Immediately, two female bears came out of the woods and killed 42 of them (2 Kings 2:23-24). The prophetic curse brought about instant doom. In your ignorance you may have also provoke an anointed man or woman of God to curse you because of your words or works. I pray that you will obtain mercy from God. Only God's mercy can release a person from the curse of a holy anointing. The Lord will have mercy on you and forgive you as you acknowledge your fault, in Jesus name. The scripture confirms that mercy overcomes judgment. I therefore announce that your judgment has been annulled in Jesus name. Go and sin no more.

Self Inflicted Curse: By now it should be obvious to you that most curses are self inflicted while others are the result of having an association with the person who is curse either as a friend, relative or descendant. To obtain the right solution it is important to differentiate between the cause and source of a curse.

Curse by Association: Proverbs 3:33 reveals that "The curse of the Lord *is* on the house of the wicked, but He blesses the home of the just." Because of one wicked person, God can curse the entire family and because of one just person He can bless the entire family. The practicality of this scripture is illustrated in one of the encounters of God's people on the way to the promise land. God through Joshua, commanded the entire camp of Israel to abstain from all the accursed things found in Jericho (Joshua 6:18). He warned that anyone who steals any of the accursed things wound be cursed and would also bring a curse upon the camp of Israel. So you see, like a communicable disease, a curse is transmissible. If you touch an accursed thing, you become cursed by transmission and anyone who comes in contact with you will also become cursed. Unfortunately, Achan the son of Carmi, was greedy and did not heed the warning. He stole some of the accursed things and brought a cursed upon the entire camp of Israel. They later went out to war against a significantly smaller city of Ai. A battle that should have been an easy win became a death trap for the children of Israel. They were disgracefully defeated by the enemy. Whenever you experience defeat or failure in a situation that should otherwise be an easy win, it could be that someone in your life has touch an accursed thing or was cursed by the sources we've previously discussed and then the person came in contact with you. You may be suffering from someone's sinful greed. Some people are not succeeding because of the accursed thing in the life of their spouse or parents. If you are in this situation, get ready to obtain your deliverance. The anointing of God coming at you as you read this book will liberate you in Jesus name.

> *Now Joshua sent men from Jericho to Ai, which is beside Beth Aven, on the east side of Bethel, and spoke to them, saying, "Go up and spy out the country." So the men went up and spied out Ai. And they returned to Joshua and said to him, "Do not let all the people go up, but let about two or three thousand men go up and attack Ai. Do not weary all the people there, for the people of Ai are few." So about three thousand men went up there from the people, but they fled before the men of Ai. And the men of Ai struck down about thirty-six men, for they chased them from before the gate as far as Shebarim, and struck them down on the descent; therefore the hearts of the people melted and became like water.*
>
> *Joshua 7:2-5*

> *So the LORD said to Joshua: "Get up! Why do you lie thus on your face? Israel has sinned, and they have also transgressed My covenant which I commanded them. For they have even taken some of the accursed things, and have both stolen and deceived; and they have also put it among their own stuff. Therefore the children of Israel could not stand before their enemies, but turned*

> *their backs before their enemies, because they have become doomed to destruction. Neither will I be with you anymore, unless you destroy the accursed from among you.*

Joshua 7:10-12

From the passage above, God declared that Israel had sinned, but only one person actually sinned as you will shortly see. The covenant God had with His people was broken because of the offence of one man. The consequence of taking the accurse thing and breaking the covenant was defeat at the hands of the weakest enemy and failure before the smallest challenge. The remedy was to destroy the accursed thing that was in the midst of the camp and everyone who was connected to it. If you have any of the accursed thing in your possession, God cannot fight for you or favor you. You must release and destroy the accursed thing. What is the accursed thing? Whatever you have stolen from someone else is an accursed thing. Any idol or charm that you carry with you where ever you go or set up in a special place in your house is an accursed thing. You must get rid of it quickly before you can experience victory and success.

> *And Achan answered Joshua and said, "Indeed I have sinned against the LORD God of Israel, and this is what I have done: When I saw among the spoils a beautiful Babylonian garment, two hundred shekels of silver, and a wedge of gold weighing fifty shekels, I coveted them and took them. And there they are, hidden in the earth in the midst of my tent, with the silver under it."*

Joshua 7:20-21

> *Then Joshua, and all Israel with him, took Achan the son of Zerah, the silver, the garment, the wedge of gold, his sons, his daughters, his oxen, his donkeys, his sheep,*

> *his tent, and all that he had, and they brought them*
> *to the Valley of Achor. And Joshua said, "Why have*
> *you troubled us? The LORD will trouble you this day."*
> *So all Israel stoned him with stones; and they burned*
> *them with fire after they had stoned them with stones.*

> *Joshua 7:24-25*

The greatest tragedy is that the innocent members of Achan's family are also held accountable for his sin. His sons, daughters, animals and all his possessions were stoned and burnt in order to purge the camp of the Lord's anger. If you are suffering from a curse by association, I pray the Lord will single you out for deliverance in the name of Jesus.

Curse by Covenant: Some people are bound together by sacred oaths or covenant in order to achieve a common goal. Depending on what their goals are, they can experience a curse or a blessing. During the time of Nehemiah, the people united with one voice to serve the Lord and took an oath of a curse if they failed to do so (Nehemiah 10: 1-29). In Acts 23:12, a group of Jews bonded together by an oath, which they would not eat or drink until they had killed Paul the Apostle. In Genesis chapter eleven the people with one accord decided to build a sky scrapper, called the tower of Babel, which would reach up to heaven. The Jews with one voice requested the release of Barabbas over Jesus Christ. They went to the extent of cursing themselves by saying, "His blood be upon us and our children" (Matthew 27:25). These are examples of curses by covenant. You take an oath as a group and placing a curse on every member of the group to establish a unified purpose of on one or more members who break the oath. This is a common practice among people who are in secret societies. That is why it is very difficult to get out of those societies without experiencing adverse consequences. If you have a difference in opinion later or attempt to resign, you face the consequence of curse of the covenant. Other members of your family may also be attacked by reason of association. It is therefore better not to enter secret societies, cults and certain fraternities, because getting out scot free is rarely possible. As you will see shortly, bonding together under a covenant creates soul ties, so even when you think you have moved far away from where the society is located, you can still be traced by your soul ties. The remedy in this case is to sever the soul tie.

> **You shall make no covenant with them, nor with their gods.**
>
> **They shall not dwell in your land, lest they make you sin against Me. For *if* you serve their gods, it will surely be a snare to you."**
>
> **Exodus 23:32-33**

Worse sins and their consequences: One sin is not equal to another and similar sins may not carry the same penalty, depending on the person committing the sin. Jesus said that anyone knowing the Father's will and yet committing an offense will get more strips than the person who offended without knowing the Father's will, for to whom much is given, much shall be required (Luke 12:47-48). God referred to the sin of Sodom and Gomorrah as being "very grave" (Genesis 18:20), due to their depravity and wickedness. John the beloved informed that there are "sins leading to death" and there are "sins that do not lead to death".

> **If anyone sees his brother sinning a sin *which does* not *lead* to death, he will ask, and He will give him life for those who commit sin not *leading* to death. There is sin *leading* to death. I do not say that he should pray about that. All unrighteousness is sin, and there is sin not *leading* to death.**
>
> **1John 5:16-17**

Clearly, the Bible in its entirety teaches that all unrighteousness is sin. But most important is that there are certain sins that have worse consequence than others and may cause serious problems in the sinner's life and in the life of those associated with him, even to the third and fourth generation. Let's consider three of the worst sins imaginable and see if you've participated in any of these "very grave sins".

Idolatry: Of course, the First commandment of the Ten Commandment is "you shall have no other gods before Me" (Exodus 20:3). The worship and celebration of other deity is the worst sin you can commit. It produces a curse that flows to the third and fourth generation (Exodus 20:5). Study scripture very well. Everyone who openly and worse yet deliberately choose to serve other gods instead of the living God, lived depraved lives and died shameful death.

Idolatry also include the use of witchcraft and sorcery as a means to an end or seeking after familiar spirits and mediums for assistance or being one yourself.

> **Give no regard to mediums and familiar spirits; do not seek after them, to be defiled by them: I *am* the LORD your God.**
>
> **Leviticus 19:31**

> **A man or a woman who is a medium, or who has familiar spirits, shall surely be put to death; they shall stone them with stones. Their blood *shall be* upon them.'"**
>
> **Leviticus 20:27**

Shedding of Blood: Numbers chapter 35 and verse 33 says "So you shall not pollute the land where you are; for blood defiles the land, and no atonement can be made for the land, for the blood that is shed on it, except by the blood of him who shed it". Murder is a great sin before God. No one has the right to take another person's life. You will be punished severely if you do so. Everyone who conspires to kill another person will not escape judgment. Haman's attempt to destroy Mordecai is a good example. Perventure you now become born again before the judgment of death catches up to you, deliverance must be sought. One of the most ungodly forms of murder is the act of abortion, the killing of embryos any time between conception and birth. There has been so much argument to justify this act, but the fact of the matter is the when abortion is committed, blood is being shed. Whether you consider the embryo a living organism or not, if you commit abortion or if you administer the abortion, you have shed innocent blood. I have counseled women who have committed abortion, some come for prayers because they are now unable to conceive, others experience depression and post traumatic stress from the procedure, while a few yet feel no remorse. Abortion is not only the act of destroying a life, but a generation and a lineage. I counseled a Hispanic woman who committed abortion as a teenager. It was a boy. She was in her early thirties when we met and at that time she had a baby girl who was about six years old. She wanted more children but could not carry her pregnancies to term. She had three miscarriages along the way. The interesting part of her story was that she often had dreams of the baby boy she had aborted when she was a teenager. This often depressed her until she was prayed for to be delivered. Her deliverance was enhanced because she was repentant.

Sexual Atrocities: Consider Leviticus 18:6-29;
'None of you shall approach anyone who is near of kin to him, to uncover his nakedness: I *am* the LORD. [7] The nakedness of your father or the nakedness of your mother you shall not uncover. She *is* your mother; you shall not uncover her nakedness. [8] The nakedness of your father's wife you shall not uncover; it *is* your father's nakedness. [9] The nakedness of your sister, the daughter of your father, or the daughter of your mother, *whether* born at home or elsewhere, their nakedness you shall not uncover. [10] The nakedness of your son's daughter or your daughter's daughter, their nakedness you shall not uncover; for theirs *is* your own nakedness. [11] The nakedness of your father's wife's daughter, begotten by your father—she *is* your sister—you shall not uncover her nakedness. [12] You shall not uncover the nakedness of your father's sister; she *is* near

of kin to your father. [13] You shall not uncover the nakedness of your mother's sister, for she *is* near of kin to your mother. [14] You shall not uncover the nakedness of your father's brother. You shall not approach his wife; she *is* your aunt. [15] You shall not uncover the nakedness of your daughter-in-law—she *is* your son's wife—you shall not uncover her nakedness. [16] You shall not uncover the nakedness of your brother's wife; it *is* your brother's nakedness. [17] You shall not uncover the nakedness of a woman and her daughter, nor shall you take her son's daughter or her daughter's daughter, to uncover her nakedness. They *are* near of kin to her. It *is* wickedness. [18] Nor shall you take a woman as a rival to her sister, to uncover her nakedness while the other is alive.

[19] 'Also you shall not approach a woman to uncover her nakedness as long as she is in her *customary* impurity. [20] Moreover you shall not lie carnally with your neighbor's wife, to defile yourself with her. [21] And you shall not let any of your descendants pass through *the fire* to Molech, nor shall you profane the name of your God: I *am* the LORD. [22] You shall not lie with a male as with a woman. It *is* an abomination. [23] Nor shall you mate with any animal, to defile yourself with it. Nor shall any woman stand before an animal to mate with it. It *is* perversion.

[24] 'Do not defile yourselves with any of these things; for by all these the nations are defiled, which I am casting out before you. [25] For the land is defiled; therefore I visit the punishment of its iniquity upon it, and the land vomits out its inhabitants. [26] You shall therefore keep My statutes and My judgments, and shall not commit *any* of these abominations, *either* any of your own nation or any stranger who dwells among you [27] (for all these abominations the men of the land have done, who *were* before you, and thus the land is defiled), [28] lest the land vomit you out also when you defile it, as it vomited out the nations that *were* before you. [29] For whoever commits any of these abominations, the persons who commit *them* shall be cut off from among their people.

If you have been involved in any of the above described sexual experiences you are in need of deliverance because each of the described sexual contact has an associated covenant, soul tie and consequence. In one of my personal prayer sessions, I devoted one hour to pray against the spirit of homosexuality in certain neighborhoods. After this intense prayer exercise, I received demonic attacks against my health that lasted for three days. After that experience I was convinced without a doubt that the homosexual movement had a demonic origin with a global agenda. For those who practice such immoral acts the penalty is death. Listen to Leviticus 20:10-16.

> **The man who commits adultery with *another* man's wife, *he* who commits adultery with his neighbor's wife, the adulterer and the adulteress, shall surely be put to death. ¹¹ The man who lies with his father's wife has uncovered his father's nakedness; both of them shall surely be put to death. Their blood *shall be* upon them. ¹² If a man lies with his daughter-in-law, both of them shall surely be put to death. They have committed perversion. Their blood *shall be* upon them. ¹³ If a man lies with a male as he lies with a woman, both of them have committed an abomination. They shall surely be put to death. Their blood *shall be* upon them. ¹⁴ If a man marries a woman and her mother, it *is* wickedness. They shall be burned with fire, both he and they, that there may be no wickedness among you. ¹⁵ If a man mates with an animal, he shall surely be put to death, and you shall kill the animal. ¹⁶ If a woman approaches any animal and mates with it, you shall kill the woman and the animal. They shall surely be put to death. Their blood *is* upon them.**

It is unfortunate that many innocent young boys and girls are forced into sexual immorality for various reasons. If you are one of such, please seek for God's deliverance power. Many of you have become emotionally unstable and physically sick because of multiple sexual partners or illegal sexual conduct. As you read this book, God's power to cleanse from sin and to heal wounds is soaking your entire spirit, soul and body in Jesus name. You would think that the sexual misconducts described in the above Bible passage were not common issues in this day and age. Au contraire. On occasions, I have ministered to rape victims, a prostitute and girls who were molested repeated by older brothers and older male neighbors without their parent's knowledge at the time. In all cases I observed a psychological or emotional trend which could not be cured by medication. Only Jesus presented the cure. For some of them, there were demonic manifestations when they were prayed for. I have spoken with a guy who slept with two sisters, thinking it was fun, not knowing that he was destroying his future. What of homosexuals? If the truth should be told, many live in severe physical and emotional pain which most of them refuse to disclose because they want the world to believe that homosexuality is natural. Of course, many of them are very intelligent, gifted and prosperous, having received tokens from demons in exchange for their altered way of life. Only Jesus can provide true and complete freedom.

I don't have hatred for homosexuals or any human being. "For all have sinned and have fallen short of the glory of God". At the same time I do not believe that the God intends for us to tolerate sin in any form or in any society. We are to expose sin and reprove it. Light exposes what darkness conceals. A central doctrine of the Holy Scriptures is that God will not permit or tolerate the act of homosexuality no matter how nice the individual may be. Sodom and Gomorrah were destroyed primarily because of this sexual culture which is deviant to God's order and protocol Genesis 19:4-25. Homosexuality is a shameful act and a sign of a debased mind according to Romans 1: 24-28

> *Therefore God also gave them up to uncleanness, in the lusts of their hearts, to dishonor their bodies among themselves, who exchanged the truth of God for the lie,*

and worshiped and served the creature rather than the Creator, who is blessed forever. Amen.
For this reason God gave them up to vile passions. For even their women exchanged the natural use for what is against nature. Likewise also the men, leaving the natural use of the woman, burned in their lust for one another, men with men committing what is shameful, and receiving in themselves the penalty of their error which was due.

Romans. 1:24-27

Homosexuals are among those who will not inherit the kingdom of God.

Do you not know that the unrighteous will not inherit the kingdom of God?
Do not be deceived. Neither fornicators, nor idolaters, nor adulterers, nor homosexuals, nor sodomites

1 Corinthians. 6:9

But you ask, "what about adultery and fornication"? Yes adultery and fornication are sexual sins that are not tolerated by God. The difference is that there are few adulterers and fornicators who would brag and boast about their lifestyle. But as for the gay community, it has become a pride and even worse, a global movement. This makes it much more a greater offense. Sinners should not justify themselves or their actions. They should plead for mercy. Mercy from God and the society at large and afterwards, seek for help and redemption. Note this principle beloved. Any sin or behavior that produces pride and self-justification is completely demonic and satanic. The motivation arises from the pit of hell. Homosexuality is another way that satan intends to destroy the family and the societies of the world. In the days of Noah the society was polluted by hybrids of humans and fallen angels, which after the drowning flood, probably gave rise to disembodied spirits called demons today. Today, satan is expressly polluting the societies of the world with a mental craze for intimacy with the same sex. If you are possessed by such a spirit either by the conditioning of your mind or by possession, Jesus Christ commissions me to set you free. I therefore command your deliverance in Jesus name, to the shame of the devil and to the glory of God. Be loosed now in Jesus name. No longer shall your desire be towards the same sex.

As a Christian we have a duty to live right before God and to reprove sin within the Church and in the world. Jesus did not confuse love with tolerance. Now I know some of you will say that these scripture of judgment are only confined to the Old Testament. The New Testament speaks of grace. I agree that the New Testament speaks of grace. Thank God for Jesus, through Whom we receive grace and truth (John 1:16-17). In John chapter 8:1-11 a woman caught in the very act of adultery was brought to Jesus by the Scribes and Pharisees for Him to condemn according to the Law of Moses (the Old Testament). The woman was caught, so the man must have ran away and escaped. The penalty for adultery was death so the men were ready to stone the woman to death even in the absence of the second offender. Jesus permitted them to stone her under one condition, "Let he that is without sin among you cast the first stone". Every man dropped his stone and left the scene leaving Jesus and the woman. Again, I say, thank God for Jesus. This woman would have died a very painful and shameful death because of adultery. But Jesus rescued her from danger. He saved her just as He is able to save you, if you've never trusted Him for your salvation. Consider this other example found in 1 Corinthians chapter 5. A man in the Church was report to have an affair with his father's wife or his step mother. Compare this action with Leviticus 20:11. The penalty was death. Now read carefully the judgment prescribed for this sex offender in the New Testament.

> ***Deliver such a one to Satan for the destruction of the flesh, that his spirit may be saved in the day of the Lord Jesus***
>
> ***1 Corinthians 5:5***

The judgment for this man was death. If man fails to administer that punishment, God certainly will not fail to do so, unless there is repentance. The point of the matter is that a willful sin committed in this dispensation of grace carries the same penalty as prescribed under the Law. The only difference is that Jesus is able to save you when you genuinely repent from the sin and look to Him for mercy. In the early Church lying to the Holy Spirit (even when represented by the man of God) carried the death sentence. Ananias and Sapphira were the first to experience this form of judgement, even though they were under the dispensation of grace (Acts 5:1-11).

Remedy for Curses: Repentance is necessary for you to obtain mercy (Proverb 28:13) and mercy will triumphs over judgment (James 2:13). The proof of repentance is confession of your sins to God or the person conducting the deliverance as well as a determination to forsaking the lifestyle of idolatry, murder sexual perversion or anything that may have enslaved you.

Salvation: You must be born again. Give your life to Jesus and begin to serve Him in spirit and in truth. He will substitute His righteousness for your sins, and His blessing for your curse. Some curses especially those involving covenants require a sacrifice for their atonement. Jesus is that sacrifice. In 2nd Samuel 21, we are told that king Saul during his reign killed the Gibeonites, whom he should not have killed because Joshua had made a covenant with them that they would not be harmed (Joshua 9:3-15). God therefore cursed the land with a famine for three years. David the reigning king enquired and was told by the Lord that the only remedy was to seven men of Saul's household. This story again illustrates how you may be suffering for another person's offence that you know nothing of. You may have never even met or seen the person and now you are paying the price for his/her errors. Saul shed innocent blood and the penalty was death. Not his death, because he was already dead at the appointed time of judgment. His blood descendants must therefore pay the price. Beloved, the good news is that Jesus has died for you. You do not have to die if you trust Him for your salvation. He was made a curse so that you can be set free from the power of the curse (Galatians 3:13).

Personal Deliverance from Corporate Curse: Some families or societies may be under a great curse that there may not be remedy for everyone, unless of course they all give their lives to Jesus. This is unusual in times past as well as in this day and age. In such a situation seek to deliver yourself first. Once your delivered you will be in a better position to deliver others. In Ezekiel 14, God said that when He sends a curse upon a land or society because of idolatry and unfaithfulness towards Him, even if Noah Daniel and Job were in that land, each would only deliver himself. Beloved, deliver yourself first at all cost. Don't continue to suffer with the masses because of ignorance. Rahab, the harlot of Jericho believed the spies sent by Joshua. She knew Jericho and all its inhabitants would be destroyed. She did not accept the verdict given to the masses but by faith connected with those who were able to deliver her and her household (Joshua 6:15). You can do the same. By faith and prayer, you can claim your deliverance through Christ Jesus. Don't waste away your life. Rise up to fulfill purpose.

Chapter Seven

Soul Ties

Soul tie is the connection of one or more souls or distinct personality to each other. Good and evil soul ties exist. A soul tie is a deep unseen union that is developed by two or more individuals. Good soul ties afford the benefits of peace, power and victory while evil soul ties developed by engaging in unhealthy relationship lead to addictive, manipulative and violent behaviors.

Soul tie is a word that is not found in scripture but its concept runs throughout the entire Bible. The word rapture is not found in scripture but the concept is evident, as with the word Trinity. To fully comprehend the meaning of soul tie, you need an understanding of the nature and the characteristics of the soul.

The soul of man comprises the mind, the seat of his intellectual ability and reasoning faculty. The soul of man produces emotions and affections which are conveyed through the body as expressions to the environment. When your soul is happy, sad or in love, for example, it is reflected through the body. The body in turn communicates message from the environment through physical senses to the soul.

The soul communicates verbally through the body's speech aperture, the vocal cords. Words come from the soul but the voice comes from the body.

The human soul was designed to fellowship, interact and bond with other spiritual and physical entities that it may be attracted to. Interaction produces either positive or negative bonding. A group of people with a common purpose (Judges 20:11) or bonded by covenant as explain before will have soul ties. Lovers have soul ties (Genesis 2:24-25), cult members, Church members (Colossians 2:2) and family members (Genesis 44:30) can develop soul ties. Friends can have soul ties. David and Jonathan were committed to caring for one another and therefore developed a special bond between themselves (1 Samuel 18:1). You can even have a soul tie with the dead because the soul does not die when the body is dead. If you have a soul tie with a dead person you will often see this person or persons in your dreams. You definitely need deliverance for separation to take place and for you to live a normal life. Soul tie with the dead is re-enforced when you remain in possession of articles that belong to that dead person. Apart from deliverance you have to give up the articles, no matter how precious they are to you or how valuable they may cost.

You can be joined to God or to a demon through idol worship and occultic practices (1 Corinthians 6:17, Numbers 25:3, Psalms 106:28, Hosea 4:17). Soul ties initiated by covenants and rituals are difficult to break and may serve as channels of blessing or cursing the other party. The concept of soul ties is therefore used by God and demons to fulfill certain purpose in people's lives. Sex is a covenant act the produces a strong bond (1 Corinthians 6:16, Genesis 34:3, 2 Samuel 13:15). Even non-consented sexual act such as rape and incest may lead to a soul tie. Homosexuals are driven by a demonic soul tie. Only the unpolluted word of God can cut asunder this evil soul ties which defies shame and embarrassment. As you read this book the fire of God is burning the umbilical cord joining you to demons that are expressing their thirsts and desires through you in the name of Jesus. I cut the rope of every puppet master controlling your life through evil soul ties in Jesus name. Be free, be loosed and be delivered.

God ordained the principle and ability of soul ties to create a covering and a blessing, but as with other establishments of God, the enemy transforms the purpose to destroy men's lives. In John 14:28, Jesus said that His Father is greater than Him even though in John 10:30 He said, "I and My Father are one". Then He prays in John 17:21 that those who will believe in Him will be one as He and the Father are one. Regarding the Spirit, the third person of the Trinity, we read that He proceeds from the Father (John 15:26) and will glorify Jesus by taking what is His and declaring it to us (John 16:14-15). The Trinity is a pure and holy Soul Tie. The Father, Son and Holy Spirit are three individual personalities which are united in purpose. Even though They are united, there is hierarchy. The Father is greater. In every soul tie, there must be one who is greater. As the Spirit proceeds forth from the greater member so also virtue, power blessing, anointing will flow from the Lord to us through His Spirit or from a leader to those who submit to him. On the contrary, in evil soul ties curses, sickness and various types of evil may proceed from the greater member to those who are enslaved by him. When you submit or solicit the assistance of an occultic practitioner, you are submitting to the demon that is at work in his life. A channel of connection has been made between you and the medium. You need deliverance immediately, because once connected to them, you are constantly under their radar.

The Purpose of Soul Ties:

- To create unity of vision, mission and purpose. The Bible confirms that two people or groups cannot productively advance unless there is a binding agreement between them. The agreement represents a written or verbal covenant or an understanding that will govern their relationship or interaction

(Amos 3:3, Psalm 133:1). Marriage is a typical example. So is also is a business or corporate merger.

- To harness the collective potential and strength of the union producing a multiplication effect that will achieve greater results than that from a single entity. Two are better than one (Ecc. 4:9). Two united entities will accomplish exponential greater exploits than a single entity. (Deut. 32:30). This is one of the purpose of networking.

- To allow for representation (Matthew 10:1-5, 2 Kings 4:29-31). When you have a soul tie with someone, you can represent that person. A husband can represent his wife at functions and vise versa.

- To transfer virtue (2 Kings 2:11-14, Numbers 11:24-26). In Numbers 11 we see how God took out of the spirit that was in Moses and imparted it to seventy other men. This is a form of transfer of virtue which makes it possible to share abilities and authority.

- To allow partners to complement one another, to strengthen (Leviticus 26:8) one another and to defend one another.

Signs and Symptoms of Ungodly Soul Ties:

The constant desire to be with someone, usually the dominant partner of a soul tie, even when you are being physically, sexually or emotionally abused by him. This behavior may also manifest as uncontrollable thoughts about the person. These are obsessive compulsive traits.

Auditory or visual hallucination about someone with the use of medication. The person that is being seen or heard is the dominate partner of the soul tie.

You may be equipped with certain gifts and abilities but will still be used like a slave to bring gain to your masters (Acts 16:16).

Regular sexual dreams known also as wet dreams with known and unknown partners. Sometimes the assaults may be physical. You will actually feel violated. The demon spirits operating in this manner are called incubus and succubus, presenting themselves as your spirit husband or spirit wife respectively. If you have a soul tie with a spirit husband or wife, you will find it difficult to have a real natural relationship because these demons will claim you as their possession (John 4:17-18). They will go to any extent to keep you from settling down naturally, even to the point of killing your prospective suitor if he or she does not relent. You will find yourself dreaming about having a family but this never becomes reality. You will experience delay in marriage and delay in having children. You need deliverance. The only remedy is to break the demonic soul tie. I speak to your life now that as you join yourself to the Lord, you are one spirit with Him. Therefore, according to the Holy Scriptures, I cut and detach every evil connection between you and all demonic sexual partners in Jesus name. At this moment lay your hands upon your hand and say out loud seven times. "I divorce myself from my spirit husband/wife now in the name of Jesus".

Chapter Eight

The Armor Of God

The purpose of the armor of God is to fight and overcome spiritual powers of darkness and forces of evil. A good knowledge and understanding of the provision that God made for all of us who will trust Him for our salvation is crucial in the battle against enslaving powers. As earlier said, doorways are the outcome of living a carnal lifestyle, without proper self-control and submission to the influence of the Holy Spirit. The first three chapters of the epistle to the Ephesians reveals what God has done for us while the last three chapters explain how we should respond to God for what has done for us.

Essentially, you must understand that you have been redeemed by the blood of Jesus, having your sins forgiven (Eph. 1:7), leading to salvation by grace (Eph. 2:8-10). Redemption is an act of repurchasing humanity back to the original plan of God, the creator. The payment for the transaction was the precious blood of Jesus. Since blood is life, it follows that, the life of Jesus, the only perfect human ever to walk the face of the earth, the one and only God-man, was the price tag for our salvation. This is the grace of God in operation. No one is deserving. No one is worthy.

God gave Gentiles (everyone who is not a Jew) access to His covenants of promise through the blood of Jesus (Eph. 2:12-13), thereby making peace between Jew and Gentile by giving both access to God by the same Spirit (Eph. 2:16-18). Salvation originated with the Jews (John 4:22), but the redemptive work of Jesus Christ equates the Gentiles with the Jews allowing them to have access to God's covenants and His precious promises in the same ways as the Jews. Salvation is the first indication of the potential for a person to limit satanic influence in his life by the operation of the Holy Spirit because you are no longer owned by the devil. God owns you now, not the devil. You can therefore renounce and resign from any secret society or cult without fear of evil consequences, because of the blood of Jesus that paid for the transfer of ownership. Please understand that your response to God for saving and redeeming you will ultimately determine the measure of grace and power that will be made available for you to live a victorious life free from demonic enslavement. The powers of darkness will not let you go without a fight. So, you should be prepared for battle as you take your stand in the victory that Jesus won for those who will believe in Him. How do you prepare for battle when the victory has been won, you may ask? The answer is simple. Not everyone is aware of the battle that Jesus fought or of the victory that He won. You may believe in Him as your savior, but if you do not realize that He came to set the captives free from bondage and to destroy the powers of darkness at work in this present dispensation, you will not know your position and potential.

- Through Jesus, God delivered us from the power of darkness and moved us to a new kingdom Col. 1: 13

- Jesus is the head of all principalities and powers Col. 2:10

- Jesus disarmed and triumph over all principalities and powers Col. 2:15

- Jesus is seated at the right hand of God, far above principalities, powers, might, dominion, and every name known to mankind Eph. 1: 20-21

- The grace of God saved us, resurrected us from dead works and made us to seat with Jesus in the heavenly places Eph. 2:1-6

- You are therefore positioned above the forces that have been working against you

You should therefore respond to God's grace firstly by walking in love and unity with others because faith works by love (Gal. 5:6). You should walk in love and unity with other believers in Christ (Eph. 4:3, 5:2) because you are not better than anyone else when it comes to being qualified for salvation. As you yield to the Holy Spirit that was deposited in after when you were saved, His character (fruits of the Spirit) will flow through you. The fruit of the Spirit is love, joy, peace, longsuffering, kindness, goodness, faithfulness, gentleness, and self-control (Gal. 5:22).

As the fruit of the Spirit blossoms in your life, you then need to engage in active ministry by identifying your gift and calling (Eph. 4:1, 7, 11-13). You are unique amongst God's creation, therefore, your gift and calling will be unique based on your inherent nature. For example, there are many gifted teachers, but no two of them will have the exact same depth of knowledge or style of communication and delivery. There are many gifted singers and musician, but no two of them will have the exact same voice quality or instrumental skill. This is true for every area of one's gifting and calling. You may operate in a similar gift as your teacher, mentor or instructor, but there will always be elements of differences. Nevertheless, understand that you were saved to serve. Whatever gift God deposited in you is meant to edify and bless people in ways that no one else can bless them.

As you grow in grace and knowledge, you should not associate with darkness or go back to your old ways of life. Rather, you should continue to live in righteousness and in holiness (Eph. 5:11). This gives evidence to the presence of the fruit of the Spirit as well as the power of the Spirit in your life (Eph. 5:18). These are the underlying principles for putting on the Armor of God because you can't keep grudge and malice or be in hatred and live an unholy life, lacking anointing, and expect adequate protection from God's armor.

> *Finally, my brethren, be strong in the Lord and in the power of His might. Put on the whole armor of God, that you may be able to stand against the wiles of the devil. For we do not wrestle against flesh and blood, but against principalities, against powers, against the rulers of the darkness of this age, against spiritual hosts of wickedness in the heavenly places. Therefore, take up the whole armor of God, that you may be able to withstand in the evil day, and having done all, to stand.*
>
> *Stand therefore, having girded your waist with truth, having put on the breastplate of righteousness, and having shod your feet with the preparation of the gospel of peace; above all, taking the shield of faith with which you will be able to quench all the fiery darts of the wicked one. And take the helmet of salvation, and the sword of the Spirit, which is the word of God; praying always with all prayer and supplication in the Spirit, being watchful to this end with all perseverance and supplication for all the saints..*
>
> *Eph. 6:10-18*

"Finally my brethren" is a term concluding the discussion. It's as if the writer was saying, "after you've considered all I've said, let me round up with this important message. Be strong and put on the armor". It is essential for you to remember always that you cannot afford to be a spiritually weak Christian. There are many Christians that have good morals and are active church goers, yet, they are weak in faith and lacking in the knowledge and understanding of spiritual concepts needed for a victorious life.

"Be strong in the Lord". This is an instruction for you to be able to withstand great force or pressure and that you are equipped to perform demanding tasks, when needed.

If you faint in the day of adversity, your strength is small (Prov. 24:10)

The people who know their God shall be strong, and carry out great exploits (Dan. 11:32).

> *I have written to you, fathers, because you have known Him who is from the beginning. I have written to you, young men, because you are strong, and the word of God abides in you, and you have overcome the wicked one.*
>
> *1 John 2:14*

A Christian should never stop growing in grace, faith and knowledge. You should continue to go from strength to strength in your walk with the Lord (Ps. 84:7).

An armor is the metal covering formerly worn by soldiers, warriors or people in combat to protect the body in battle. The armor protects the vital parts of the body and defends the wearer from the enemy's weapons. The components of the armor and their importance are appreciated when you have a good understanding of your enemy.

> *Put on all of God's armor so that you will be able to stand firm against all strategies of the devil. For we are not fighting against flesh-and-blood enemies, but against evil rulers and authorities of the unseen world, against mighty powers in this dark world, and against evil spirits in the heavenly places.*
>
> *Eph. 6: 11-12 (NLT)*

1. The enemy is not necessarily human or physical. They are invisible evil spirits (Lk. 10:18-20).

2. Principalities or rulers: this level of evil spirits have kingdoms or dominions, thrones (Col. 1:15-6). They make rules and decisions over territories. Prince of Persia (Dan. 10:13), king of Tyre (Ezekiel. 28:12-19).

3. Powers or authorities: these are spiritual leaders with followers who worship them, because they love to be worshiped. They can be referred to as the spirit behind every deity that is worshipped. For example, Baal, Shango, Diana, etc.

4. Evil spirits in heavenly places. These represent generalized demonic presence in the atmosphere and all over the face of the earth (Eph. 2:2).

The Bible is filled with illustrations of satanic activities;
Satan stood against the nation of Israel and inspired king David to carry out a program that was clearly against the will of God (1 Chron. 21:1). Satan stood against and frustrated the efforts of Joshua the anointed high priest of his day (Zach. 3:1), demon spirits entered people and enabled them to have supernatural abilities such as strength and revelation knowledge (Lk. 8:26-31, Acts 16:16-18) or influenced the person to misbehave (Lk. 22:3), afflicted people (1 Sam. 16:14, Matt. 17: 14-17), lied through people (1 King 22:19-23) and cause all manner of sickness and diseases (Matt. 4:24). The story of Job as told in the book of Job chapters 1 and 2 summarizes the devastation the satan and his cohorts can cause, if permitted by God. He destroyed Job's business, killed all ten of his children and afflicted his body with an incurable disease. Job, a righteous man, was made to experience great physical and emotional pain. Many people in the world today are going through tragedy, havoc and pain because of satanic operations in their lives.

For divine security and protection, you should "put on the whole armor of God". Not some parts of the armor but all of the armor. The armor is made up of 6 parts.

1. Waist belt of truth; truth is knowing the true God and not serving any other god with Him (1 Jn. 5:18-21). Knowledge of the truth initiates freedom (Jn. 8:32). Ultimately, the truth is knowing God and keeping His commandments (1Jn. 2:4)

2. Breastplate of righteousness; Jesus is your righteousness but as an action, righteousness is doing the right thing and refusing to do the wrong thing (Is. 59:17). Joseph refused to fornicate with his master's wife (Gen. 39:7-10). Abraham believed God and was willing to offer up his promised child, Isaac. This was account to him as righteousness (Rom. 4:3)

3. Shoe, Sandal, or Boots on your feet; this is a deliberate attempt to spreading the gospel of Jesus Christ and to testify of His goodness and power in your life (Isa. 52:7, Rev. 12:11). By witnessing, you are shaming the devil and giving glory to God. David practiced this when he confronted Goliath and the Lord gave him victory. He testified of the power of God and how God had previously delivered him. The three Hebrew's did the same before Nebuchadnezzar and God vindicated them (Dan. 3:15-26)

4. Shield of faith; because many battles originate in the mind, your thoughts and belief play a major role in your response to the enemy's attacks. Faith shields the mind from words philosophy and heretical doctrines that can pollute and derail you. Faith is seated in the mind. When your mind is full of faith, you have confidence towards God (1 Jn. 3:21), but when you lack faith, fear takes over. For this reason, you should constantly renew your mind with the word of God to build up your faith (Rom. 10:17). Faith gives victory (1 Jn. 5:4).

5. Helmet of salvation; you must be genuinely saved (Is. 59:17). Your salvation should not be guessed. You have to be certain and confident that you are saved by grace. You should know beyond a reasonable doubt that you belong to God and that you are one of the sheep in His pasture (Jn. 10:27). As a good Shepherd, He will protect and provide for you as long as you trust Him (Ps. 23).

6. Sword of the Spirit, which is the word of God; The word is a powerful tool of offense. It works with faith because to speak or confess what you believe (Rom. 10:17, 2 Cor. 4:13). The word is alive and it is very powerful (Jn. 6:63, Heb. 4:12). It can impact both the spiritual and physical realm. Salvation begins with your confession. Your spiritual growth is influenced by your knowledge of scripture. Obtaining victory in the battles of life is dependent on your use of the word of God that is stored in your heart. Let the word of God dwell in you richly (Col. 3:16)!

Chapter Nine

Channels Of Deliverance

Obtaining deliverance requires warfare. An obsessive, suppressive, oppressive or possessive demon or power will not let you go willingly without a fight. Jesus said, "no one can enter a strong man's house and plunder his goods, unless he first bind the strong man" (Mark 3:27). And again, "when an unclean spirit goes out of a man, he goes through dry places, seeking rest; and finding none, he says, ""I will return to my house from which I came"". And when he comes, he finds it swept and put in order. Then he goes and takes with him seven other spirits more wicked than himself, and they enter and dwell here; and the last state of that man is worse than the first" (Luke 11:24-26). Please note that these evil spirits have individual personalities (Jesus refers to the spirit as "he" and not "it"), they desire to claim ownership (I will return to my house), have measure different measures of wickedness and strength (seven other spirits more wicked than he).

Think of it as two nations. The smaller nation is you and you have been colonized by a larger and stronger nation. You will have to desperately fight for your independence through legislature and the use of force. Some Empires colonize smaller territories for decades and even centuries because of the benefit that they are deriving from the smaller territory. Demons derive their benefit by demonstrating their powers against the host or expressing themselves through the host. Once the benefit is gone and the territory becomes a liability for the Empire, it is discarded. Demons operate by the same principle. Their activities continue in the victim's life until they no longer derive the desired benefit, thereafter, the victim is destroyed and the demons go on to another territory. Demonic activity may continue for days, weeks, months, years and even a life time. It may even continue from one generation to the next in a family or skip a generation and continue in the third generation, similar to the principle of dominance and recessive traits in genetics. Unless you stand up for your right and demand your freedom through Christ Jesus, your life will be under the influence of these terrible and merciless agents. In Christ, greater is He that is in you than he that is in the world. This is the indwelling presence of the Holy Spirit and His anointing upon your life.

Warfare requires the use of weaponry, whether they are bow, arrows, bullets, missiles, thunders and lightening. The Bible teaches that our weapons of warfare are not physical but mighty in God to pull down spiritual strongholds, because we are not battling against flesh and blood (2 Corinthians 10:3-4, Ephesians 6:10-12). Remember that as in the physical so it is in the spirit realm. The physical weapons that we see have counterparts in the spirit. Have you ever had a dream whereby someone hits you in the face and when you wake up, behold, your lips are swollen. Or you dream of being in a fight and when you wake up, you feel fatigued and sore. Consider Jacob, who fought with an Angel. The angel dislodged his hip in the dream and behold when he woke up he began to limp (Gen. 32:32). Many lives have been terminated because they were shot in their dreams while others encounter accidents after dreaming of such. The conclusion is that spiritual weapons are very real. They are at your disposal. Make use of them.

Spiritual Weapons

Apart from the name of Jesus, which is greater than every other name in heaven, on earth, in hell, beneath the land and sea, and which gives us authority to stand as He stood, there are three must have principal weapons in any spiritual warfare. All others are secondary.

The Blood of Jesus: Every child of God should regularly confess his position and covering to be the blood of Jesus. This blood represents the life of God containing supernatural immune factors to ward off demons and adversity in a similar way that natural blood has defensive agents against external and internal disease causing agents. As natural blood has wound healing factors, so does the Blood of Jesus and this property may be appropriated by drinking wine or grape juice that has been sanctified to represent the blood of Jesus in the act of Holy Communion. It is therefore wise to take Communion regularly when you're sick or possessed (Jn. 6:56). When you are covered by the blood the following scripture becomes real; "for you are dead and your life is hid with Christ in God." Colossians 3:3. Every deliverance minister should bring himself under the covering of the blood before attempting a deliverance session. Failure to do so may result in injury due to demonic counter attacks. Confessing coverage of the blood of Jesus is not enough, you must live right. Remember the seven sons of Sceva in Acts 19:13-16. Demons know who you are and whether or not you are in Christ. You may show off in front of people but the fact is that you're true identity is known in the spirit realm. In this realm, which is invisible to the naked eye, everyone's identity is revealed in one of two formats. You either are a light or you're darkness. If you are therefore in Christ, the light of the glory of God radiates through you. But if you're not in Christ, you have no light in you. Only darkness. So anyone who is given the grace to see into the spirit realm will clearly discern the type of spirits in operation. Since everyone is not given this grace, discernment in the physical environment requires testing the spirit of an individual by the words they speak and the fruit they manifest.

The Word of God: The word is the sword of the Spirit for all believers to use (Ephesians 6:17, Hebrews 4:12). God delivers by His word and has enabled us to speak as His oracles (Psalm 107:20, I Peter 4:11). The word compares to a hammer and to fire depending on the need of the hour (Jeremiah 23:29). The word should be confesses regularly and prayed in faith. Then it will produce results. Without faith, the word is powerless. Believe what you say and say what you believe. Use Biblical examples that are relevant to the situation at hand. When addressing demons always say, it is written or the Lord says or according to the word of God, such and such. Jesus conversed with the devil and overcame him with the word of God (Matthew 4:1-11). Go and do likewise in Jesus name.

The Anointing: Jesus was manifested to destroy the works of the devil (1 John 3:8). Jesus became manifest after He was anointed with the power of the Holy Spirit. He went into the wilderness full of the Spirit, fasted forty days and nights, overcame the temptations of the devil, and then came out in the power (or the anointing) of the Holy Spirit (Luke 4:1-14). There is always a price to pay for the anointing. Salvation is free, but the anointing comes with a personal price. You're indwelt by the Spirit once you're saved but you are empowered by the Spirit when you are fire baptized. Prayer, fasting and transfer of the anointing by the laying on of hands are essential for receiving the anointing of the Holy Ghost. Once received you are licensed to silence evil voices and cast out demons hiding in secure places. The anointing also allows for the demonstration of spiritual gifts categorized as inspirational, revelation and power gifts (1 Corinthians 12:7-11). The anointing destroys the yoke in people's lives and lift burdens from those who are oppressed Isaiah 10:27). The anointing of God is so dynamic that it cannot be limited and it can work through other channels such as songs and musical instruments (1 Samuel 16:23) olive oil (Mark 6:13, James 5:14), sanctified water, prayer cloth and handkerchief (Acts 19:11-12).

The Name of Jesus: "In My name they will cast out demons" (Mark 16:17)". The name is not magical. It is miraculous. The power behind the name is not in the word or the spelling or the pronunciation. The power behind the name lies in the person it represents. When you speak or command in the name of Jesus, it is as if Jesus were the one speaking. So it's not the name but the person that the name represent. Understand that Jesus is the Greek form of the Hebrew name "Joshua" or "Yesuwah". So if you pray in the name of "Joshua", "Yesuwah", "Jesus", "Jesu" etc., your prayers will be answered if you believe. Even though the name may be called in different languages, it is the person represented by the name that is important. The person praying must have faith in the Person represented by the name. Listen, in the days of Jesus our Lord, there were others who were called Jesus as well. As a matter of fact, Jesus or the Hebrew, Joshua was given to a few Old Testament men of God, two of which are very prominent. Joshua (formerly called Hoshea [Numbers 13:16]) the son of Nun, Moses assistant (Numbers 11:28) and Joshua the high priest (Zechariah 3:1) during the days of Zerubbabel, governor of Judah (Zechariah 4:6). So in the days of Jesus (Matthew 1:21), there were others with the same name. For this reason Jesus the Lord was differentiated from the others by calling Him Jesus of Nazareth (Matthew 21:11, 26:71, Mark 10:47) or Jesus the Christ. Even demons referred to the Lord as Jesus of Nazareth, the Holy One of God (Mark 1: 23-24). No other Jesus could have answered to the title.

In the school of deliverance, not everyone can utilize the name of Jesus and expect to get miraculous results. Some including the sons of Sceva, a Jewish chief priest desired to use the name to cast out devils (Acts 19: 13-16). They had no relationship with Jesus but thought they could cast out devils as Paul and other believers did. The evil spirit responded that "Jesus I know, Paul I know, but who are you"? Instead of the evil spirit to come out of the possessed man, he leaped on and overpowered the imposters who were using the name of Jesus illegally. That's right. If you do not have a relationship with Jesus, you are using His name illegally and the name will not work for you in the area of deliverance. It may work in other situations such as a cry for God's mercy or provision, but not in deliverance when it comes to dealing with demons personally. Demons do not answer to people who are spiritual imposters. Remember, they can tell the different. Even if you're saved, I do not encourage you to minister deliverance to someone if you know that you're living in sin. If you do, you are setting yourself up for a backlash and counter attack. First settle your issue with God before you stand in the gap for others. Keep in mind the doorways previously discussed. Sin opens the door for all forms of evil.

Also, beware that evil spirits can say the name of Jesus. Some people teach that they cannot. Some teach that whenever the name of Jesus is mentioned all evil spirits fall and tremble. Keep in mind that it depends on who is using the name. We have seen in various scriptures that evil spirits recognize Jesus, and even say His name (Mark 1: 23-24, Acts 19: 13-16). Don't let this surprise you. They still have to obey whatever command is given them in that powerful name, when a right standing speaks to them in Jesus name.

By inference, a demon possessed person can come to Church regular, and be part of prayer meetings using the name of Jesus and yet not surrender or be exposed to others in the congregation. This is where the anointing makes the difference. A man possessed with evil spirits came to the Synagogue time after time but when Jesus came into that Synagogue and as He taught with authority, the evil spirit cried out and was exposed (Mark 1: 22-27). The anointing exposed the evil spirit. Our Churches should be charged with the anointing of the Holy Ghost. Devils are uncomfortable in the atmosphere of the anointing but they are comfortable in luke-warm and passive Churches. I pray that as you read this book, you will receive demon exposing anointing in Jesus name. Anyone possessed by evil spirits will not be comfortable in your presence in Jesus name!

Other channels for deliverance include the following;

Laying on of Hands: "They will lay hands on the sick and they will recover" (Mark 16:18). Laying on of hands is one of the channels of impartation. It is not only used in deliverance but in any situation where there's a need to transfer virtue and anointing. The practice of laying on of hands originated in the Old Testament and is still very relevant today. For example, God told Moses to lay his hands on Joshua and release some of his authority for Joshua to operate (Numbers 27: 18-20). Elisha place his hands on the hands of the king of Israel thereby releasing an impartation into his life to be victorious over the king of Syria (2 Kings 13:16).

In the New Testament, Jesus laid hands on the mother in-law of Peter and she immediately recovered of fever (Matthews 8:14), new converts in Samaria received the Holy Spirit by the laying on of hands of Peter and John (Acts 8: 17), Ananias the disciple laid hands on Saul (who became Paul) when he was blind and Saul received his sight (Acts 9:17), Paul laid hands on a man sick with fever and dysentery and the man was healed (Acts 28:8). No doubt that laying on of hands is an act of faith and is a useful tool for deliverance. Always keep in mind that anointing and virtue flow from the person who is filled to the person who is empty or in need of healing or deliverance. This is similar to the process of osmosis where water flows through a membrane into a solution of higher solute concentration thereby equalizing the concentrations of the two media. This fact is important to note because someone with faith and understanding can deliberately touch you and draw virtue from you without your consent. This was the case between Jesus and the woman with the issue of blood (Luke 8: 42-44). There were many people who were touching Jesus by pressing against Him in the crowd but none drew out virtue except for the woman with the blood disease. By faith and determination she drew virtue for her healing out of the Master. Immediately Jesus knew that virtue had been release from Him because He felt drained. The first sign of the release of virtue is exhaustion depending on the amount of virtue released. When virtue goes out of you, you must go back to the presence of God for replenishment and refilling.

Men of God should be careful of who they touch or who touch them. Satanic agents can touch a man or woman of God in an unsuspecting manner in order to draw virtue thereby causing that minister of God to grow spiritually weak. For this reason, it is recommended that a minister of God, especially one who operates in the deliverance ministry go before the Lord daily for replenishment of virtue and anointing. Conversely, a child of God should not allow just any minister to lay hands on them. The one you allow to lay hands on you should be someone you know and trust. And if you don't know him personally, talk to God first and seek for a conviction within your heart. And if you're not sure what to do, plead the blood of Jesus over your body, soul and spirit before you subject yourself to the ministration of the laying on of hands of a stranger. Many false prophets and false teachers have gone into the world and are going around Churches siphoning virtue and glory from unsuspecting believers by the principle of laying on of hands. They fully understand that by laying their evil anointed hands on your head or body, they can transmit their nature into you or draw good virtue and glory from you. Child of God, please beware. Your life is precious and should not be wasted.

Fervent Prayer and prolonged Fasting: When the disciples could not deliver an epileptic from the possessive spirit. Jesus performed the deliverance and revealed to them that some types of spirit will not come out except by prayer and fasting (Mark 9:29). At times deep rooted spirits require fasting for days for them to loosen their grips or be cast out. This is evident in those with sickness of demonic origin or who are afflicted as a consequence of evil covenants and curses. The following chapter will be devoted to prayer points against sin, sickness, curses, evil covenants and maintaining deliverance.

The influence of a Mediator: Psalm 106:23and Hosea 12:10-12 explain the role of a mediator in the deliverance of others. A mediator intercedes on behalf of the people. Everyone occupying one of the five fold ministerial offices is called of God to be a mediator in one form or the other to those submissive to him. Moses was the mediator of deliverance of the people of Israel out of the bondage of Egypt. Many of the prophets and Apostles of Bible days were vessels of deliverance for others. The same principle applies today. We are still living in the New Testament dispensation where the Holy Spirit is at work through those who believe in Christ. As a mediator delivering one who is oppresses or possessed, you may lay hands on the victim to liberate him in the name of Jesus (Mark 16:17) or speak authoritatively to command the devil to release or come out of the victim.

Corporate Anointing: Jesus encourages corporate prayer and James request we pray for one another (Matthew 18:18-19, James 5:16). As the Church gathered and prayed continuously for Peter, God sent an angel to deliver him from prison (Acts. 12)

Anointed Materials: Prayer cloth/handkerchief (Acts 19:11-12) and anointing oil (Mark 6:13) are but a few of the materials you may be led of the Spirit to use in conducting deliverance. It is not uncommon for the Holy Spirit to lead you to use water, sand, spit, wood, your shadow etc. God is obviously very creative. He is not limited by means or channels. Although it is essential to warn you to be sure that what is done is of the Holy Spirit and there are scriptures to support the action. There are many false prophets and teachers in the world today who are counterfeiting the work of the Holy Spirit. They are working for their bellies and the shame will be exposed after a short while.

When conducting a deliverance session, the minister should cover himself and others around with the blood of Jesus. Then let the deliverance candidate confess his sins and surrender to God through Christ. Lead him through the sinner's prayer by repeating after you. The prayer may go as such;

Dear God,

I know that I have sinned. I was born in sin and have lived in sin. Today I confess my sins (ask him to confess the sins he can remember to God. He can whisper it so that no one else will hear). Please forgive me and accept me. I believe that Jesus, the Son of God died for my sins and gave me His righteousness event while I lived in sin. I promise to forsake my sins by Your grace and will live to please You. Thank You for making me Your child. I receive Your Holy Spirit into my life, in Jesus holy name.

Chapter Ten

Prayer Points For Deliverance

I believe that many of the foundational issues that are manifesting in your life can be solved by aggressively praying through the following prayer points. I have prayed these prayers points with others and they came back to testify.

Pray these prayer points at midnight, **NAKED**. You were born naked and so praying naked indicates that you are addressing your foundation. Pray alone but with fervency, ensuring that you are sweating by the time you are done. Endeavor to pray at least 3 consecutive days and then at least once a month on a day that represents you birthday. For example, if you were born on February 29th, let your midnight naked prayers be on the 29th day of every month. You may substitute February 28th on years that are not leap years.

Confess the following before you proceed.

"Praise be to God for granting me the right of an adopted child because of the finished work of salvation by Jesus Christ, His only begotten Son, on the cross of Calvary. By accepting Jesus Christ as my personal Lord and Savior, all my past sins have been nail to His cross and I am eternally forgiven. His shed blood has erased every evil ordinance written against me for my destruction. In dying, Jesus took my place in death and destroyed its power over my life. In resurrecting, Jesus affords me victory in every area of my life and over every spirit at war with my present existence. In ascending up on high, Jesus guarantees my eternity in heaven with the saints of God who have also fought the good fight of faith. I believe this with all my heart because it is the truth of the Gospel of Jesus. Praise God, Praise God, Praise God."

1. I'm a new creation. Old things are past away according to 2 Cor. 5:17. Therefore Father, in the name of Jesus, let old deeds and habits deeply embedded in my carnal nature by stripped off of me in the name of Jesus. Holy Spirit, strip me of carnality. Blood of Jesus, flush my DNA and establish Your newness of life in me.

2. Every curse upon my life because of past sins must expire in the name of Jesus. Prov. 26:2. Because the wages of sin is a curse that produces death but the gift of God is blessing and life through grace. (Rom. 6:24, Isa. 49:24-25). I choose life and not death. I choose to be blessed and not cursed (Deut. 30:19).

3. Every evil words spoken against my life must not stand or be established. For who is he that speaks and it comes to pass if the Lord has not spoken it. It is written that the Lord has spoken blessings over my life and I shall not be cursed. (Isa. 7:7, 8:10, Num. 23:8, 23)

4. In the name of Jesus, I renounce every evil association that I have been involved with, either by blood agreement, spoken agreement or written agreement. I renounce every evil association imposed on me by virtue of inheritance or election, in the name of Jesus. For it is written, " Wherefore come out from among them, and be ye separate, saith the Lord, and touch not the unclean thing; and I will receive you." (Isa 52:11). I declare that I am on the LORD's side and I belong to Him.

5. . Because of the covering Blood of Jesus over my life, I am protect from every witchcraft arrow and manipulations in the name of Jesus. I destroy the influence of sorcery, divination, enchantments, black magic, and the likes over my life in Jesus name. For it is written, "For there is no sorcery against me, Nor any divination against me" in Jesus name (Num. 23:23).

6. I proclaim my deliverance from every cage of the enemy that has ensnared me before my salvation in the name of Jesus. Let every snare of the fowler that has captured my soul brake now by reason of the resurrection power of Jesus name (Ps. 91:3, Ps. 124:7).

7. As the LORD Jesus called out Lazarus from the grave with a thunderous shout, I call out my virtue from where ever it has been buried or hidden in the name of Jesus. "My virtue, come forth now in Jesus name. You must come forth now!)

8. Nakedness means shame. I nullify the authority of every dream in which I have seen myself naked. In the name of Jesus, instead of my shame, I shall receive double honor (Isa. 61:7).

9. I dispel every dark cloud or covering that is overshadowing my glory as well as God's glory in my life in the name of Jesus. For it is written that I will arise and shine for my light has come and the Glory of the LORD has risen upon me (Isa. 60:1).

10. According to Exodus 22:4,7,9 "For all manner of trespass, whether it be for ox, for ass, for sheep, for raiment, or for any manner of lost thing which another challenges to be his, the cause of both parties shall come before the judges; and whom the judges shall condemn, he shall pay <u>double</u> unto his neighbor", I therefore receive double for all that I've loss and for every stolen virtue in the name of Jesus. God is the righteous

Judge and He has justifies me over my enemies by faith in the finished work of Jesus.

11. {If you are the first born pray this}; I take back my birthright in the name of Jesus. I receive my inheritance as ordained by divine predestination. According to Isa. 22: "And the key of the house of David will I lay upon his shoulder; so he shall open, and none shall shut; and he shall shut, and none shall open." The key to my family is given to me and with it I unlock every door of Joy, Peace, Promotion and Success in the name of Jesus. I also lock every evil door in Jesus name.

12. In Joel 2:25, God promised me restoration by saying; "And I will restore to you the years that the locust hath eaten, the cankerworm, and the caterpillar, and the palmerworm, my great army which I sent among you." I therefore receive restoration for every year of my life that has been wasted in the area of academics, career and relationship. By divine grace I am translated to my God ordained position in the name of Jesus.

13. Affliction shall not come against me a second time in Jesus name (Nahum 1:9). I will not fall and stumble over past faults and errors in Jesus name. The errors or my father and mother will be an abomination for me in the name of Jesus.

14. I take back the Master Key of my destiny from the hands of every evil gate keeper in the name of Jesus (Acts 12:6). Let my double doors open, let my prison doors open, let my gate of inflow of blessings be opened continually in the name of Jesus (Acts. 12:10, Isa. 45:1, 60:11) .

15. Let the spirit of blindness afflict every stargazer and astrologer monitoring my destiny in the name of Jesus (Isa. 47:

16. Every diagnoses sickness in my body, hear the word of God, by the stripes of Jesus I have been healed. I receive my healing in the name of Jesus. (Isa. 53:5)

17. Every evil boil, growth and tumor within my body arising from satanic arrows and poisons, wither away now in the name of Jesus. For every seed my Father has not planted must be uprooted in Jesus name.

18. Every spirit of infirmity operating within my body, I command you to come out in Jesus name. My body is the sanctuary of the Holy Spirit and not a cave for demon spirits. Come out now, you foul spirit in Jesus name.

19. I am a carrier of God's glory (Isa. 60:1). Every situation of shame and disgrace must turn around now to favor me in Jesus name. Because I love God, all things must work together for my good in Jesus name (Rom. 8:28).

20. Let every satanic agenda for my life, my home and career be nullified in Jesus name.

21. By the Blood of Jesus, I delete every demonic program installed in my destiny.

22. The Bible says, "they will surely gather together, but not by Me", therefore let every evil network and conspiracy against my life be scattered in the name of Jesus.

23. I receive the abundance of the four corners of the earth and wealth of the gentiles in the name of Jesus (Isa. 60:5).

24. As to everything there is a season and a time for every purpose (Ecc. 3:1) I declare that my set time of favor and honor is now (Psa. 102:13).

25. No weapon fashioned against me shall prosper (Isa. 54:17), therefore, every divination, enchantment and charms will be ineffective against my life in the almighty name of Jesus. I am immune to bewitchment and enslavement by the blood of Jesus. I will therefore remain strong in the Lord and in the power of His might (Eph. 6:10).

About The Book

Bible Truth About Deliverance is a systematic "in a nutshell approach" teaching on the controversial issue of deliverance. It explores the causality of certain events as well as the remedy. The principles are undoubtedly Bible based and factual to everyday life. The Book lays emphasis with concrete examples on the influence of the spirit realm on the physical realm in a way that even the naïve person will come to see the light. Everyone will benefit from the teachings contained in this book. This version features an expanded chapter six - Curses and a new chapter eight - The Armor of God

About The Author

Born in Nigeria, West Africa, Pastor Yemi Adedeji, M.D. has had the privilege of building a successful career as a medical doctor in the field of pharmacovigilance in the United States. He is currently, Senior Medical Director and Head of Pharmacovigilance in a fast-growing East Coast Pharmaceutical Company. His life's calling and passion is to get the truth of God's word in the heart of God's people so that they may be established to fulfill God's purpose for their lives. He is founder of Peacemakers Evangelical Ministries and the Senior Pastor and Pastor in Charge of Christ Glory International Ministries, headquartered in Irvington, NJ. He is married to Pastor Shola Adedeji an anointed soloist, preacher, motivational speaker, and human rights activist in developing countries, including Nigeria. They are blessed with godly children.